THE QUEST OF THE SACRED SLIPPER

By
SAX ROHMER

The Quest Of The Sacred Slipper

by Sax Rohmer

Copyright © 2023

All Rights reserved.
No part of this publication may be reproduced, stored in a retrieval system, or transmitted in any form or by any means, electronic, mechanical, photocopying or Otherwise, without the written permission of the publisher.

The author/editor asserts the moral right to be identified as the author/editor of this work.

ISBN: 978-93-57482-60-8

Published by

DOUBLE 9 BOOKS

2/13-B, Ansari Road, Daryaganj
New Delhi – 110002
info@double9books.com
www.double9books.com
Tel. 011-40042856

This book is under public domain

ABOUT THE AUTHOR

English author Arthur Henry "Sarsfield" Ward, well known as Sax Rohmer, lived from 15 February 1883 to 1 June 1959. He is most known for the Dr. Fu Manchu book series, which stars the notorious master criminal.

Rohmer, like his contemporaries Algernon Blackwood and Arthur Machen, claimed affiliation with a Hermetic Order of the Golden Dawn group. Edgar Allan Poe, Arthur Conan Doyle, and M. P. Shiel appear to have been Rohmer's principal authors of literary inspiration.

After penning Little Tich in 1911, Richard Rohmer wrote the first Fu Manchu novel, The Mystery of Dr. Fu-Manchu, first published in a serialization from October 1912 to June 1913. Rohmer didn't return to the saga with Daughter of Fu Mancha until 1931. Stoll had successfully adapted the first three works into a pair of serials in the 1920s. He started the series for Collier's in 1930 but was unhappy with the female supervillain Head Centre at the start. Later, for the Sumuru series, he would go back to Drake Roscoe and his female supervillain. The series was criticized for creating a false image of London's Chinese community as crime-ridden.

CONTENTS

CHAPTER I
    THE PHANTOM SCIMITAR 7

CHAPTER II
    THE GIRL WITH THE VIOLET EYES 12

CHAPTER III
    "HASSAN OF ALEPPO" 15

CHAPTER IV
    THE OBLONG BOX 19

CHAPTER V
    THE OCCUPANT OF THE BOX 24

CHAPTER VI
    THE RING OF THE PROPHET 29

CHAPTER VII
    FIRST ATTEMPT ON THE SAFE 34

CHAPTER VIII
    THE VIOLET EYES AGAIN 37

CHAPTER IX
    SECOND ATTEMPT ON THE SAFE 41

CHAPTER X
    AT THE BRITISH ANTIQUARIAN MUSEUM 48

CHAPTER XI
    THE HOLE IN THE BLIND 53

CHAPTER XII
    THE HASHISHIN WATCH 55

CHAPTER XIII
    THE WHITE BEAM 57

CHAPTER XIV
    A SCREAM IN THE NIGHT 61

CHAPTER XV
    A SHRIVELLED HAND 66

CHAPTER XVI
    THE DWARF 69

CHAPTER XVII
    THE WOMAN WITH THE BASKET 74
CHAPTER XVIII
    WHAT CAME THROUGH THE WINDOW 82
CHAPTER XIX
    A RAPPING AT MIDNIGHT 85
CHAPTER XX
    THE GOLDEN PAVILION 89
CHAPTER XXI
    THE BLACK TUBE 93
CHAPTER XXII
    THE LIGHT OF EL-MEDINEH 99
CHAPTER XXIII
    THE THREE MESSAGES 103
CHAPTER XXIV
    I KEEP THE APPOINTMENT 108
CHAPTER XXV
    THE WATCHER IN BANK CHAMBERS 110
CHAPTER XXVI
    THE STRONG-ROOM 117
CHAPTER XXVII
    THE SLIPPER 120
CHAPTER XXVIII
    CARNETA 122
CHAPTER XXIX
    WE MEET MR. ISAACS 127
CHAPTER XXX
    AT THE GATE HOUSE 132
CHAPTER XXXI
    THE POOL OF DEATH 136
CHAPTER XXXII
    SIX GRAY PATCHES 140
CHAPTER XXXIII
    HOW WE WERE REINFORCED 146
CHAPTER XXXIV
    MY LAST MEETING WITH HASSAN OF ALEPPO 151

CHAPTER I
THE PHANTOM SCIMITAR

I was not the only passenger aboard the S.S. Mandalay who perceived the disturbance and wondered what it might portend and from whence proceed. A goodly number of passengers were joining the ship at Port Said. I was lounging against the rail, pipe in mouth, lazily wondering, with a large vagueness.

What a heterogeneous rabble it was!—a brightly coloured rabble, but the colours all were dirty, like the town and the canal. Only the sky was clean; the sky and the hard, merciless sunlight which spared nothing of the uncleanness, and defied one even to think of the term dear to tourists, "picturesque." I was in that kind of mood. All the natives appeared to be pockmarked; all the Europeans greasy with perspiration.

But what was the stir about?

I turned to the dark, bespectacled young man who leaned upon the rail beside me. From the first I had taken to Mr. Ahmad Ahmadeen.

"There is some kind of undercurrent of excitement among the natives," I said, "a sort of subdued Greek chorus is audible. What's it all about?"

Mr. Ahmadeen smiled. After a gaunt fashion, he was a handsome man and had a pleasant smile.

"Probably," he replied, "some local celebrity is joining the ship."

I stared at him curiously.

"Any idea who he is?" (The soul of the copyhunter is a restless soul.)

A group of men dressed in semi-European fashion—that is, in European fashion save for their turbans, which were green—passed close to us along the deck.

Ahmadeen appeared not to have heard the question.

The disturbance, which could only be defined as a subdued uproar, but could be traced to no particular individual or group, grew momentarily louder—and died away. It was only when it had completely ceased that one realized how pronounced it had been—how altogether peculiar, secret; like that incomprehensible murmuring in a bazaar when, unknown to the insular visitor, a reputed saint is present.

Then it happened; the inexplicable incident which, though I knew it not, heralded the coming of strange things, and the dawn of a new power; which should set up its secret standards in England, which should flood Europe and the civilized world with wonder.

A shrill scream marked the overture—a scream of fear and of pain, which dropped to a groan, and moaned out into the silence of which it was the cause.

"My God! what's that?"

I started forward. There was a general crowding rush, and a darkly tanned and bearded man came on board, carrying a brown leather case. Behind him surged those who bore the victim.

"It's one of the lascars!"

"No—an Egyptian!"

"It was a porter—?"

"What is it—?"

"Someone been stabbed!"

"Where's the doctor?"

"Stand away there, if you please!"

That was a ship's officer; and the voice of authority served to quell the disturbance. Through a lane walled with craning heads they bore the insensible man. Ahmadeen was at my elbow.

"A Copt," he said softly. "Poor devil!" I turned to him. There was a queer expression on his lean, clean-shaven, bronze face.

"Good God!" I said. "His hand has been cut off!"

That was the fact of the matter. And no one knew who was responsible for the atrocity. And no one knew what had become of the severed hand! I wasted not a moment in linking up the story. The pressman within me acted automatically.

"The gentleman just come aboard, sir," said a steward, "is Professor Deeping. The poor beggar who was assaulted was carrying some of the Professor's baggage." The whole incident struck me as most odd. There was an idea lurking in my mind that something else—something more—lay behind all this. With impatience I awaited the time when the injured man, having received medical attention, was conveyed ashore, and Professor Deeping reappeared. To the celebrated traveller and Oriental scholar I introduced myself.

He was singularly reticent.

"I was unable to see what took place, Mr. Cavanagh," he said. "The poor fellow was behind me, for I had stepped from the boat ahead of him. I had just taken a bag from his hand, but he was carrying another, heavier one. It is a clean cut, like that of a scimitar. I have seen very similar wounds in the cases of men who have suffered the old Moslem penalty for theft."

Nothing further had come to light when the Mandalay left, but I found new matter for curiosity in the behaviour of the Moslem party who had come on board at Port Said.

In conversation with Mr. Bell, the chief officer, I learned that the supposed leader of the party was one, Mr. Azraeel. "Obviously," said Bell, "not his real name or not all it. I don't suppose they'll show themselves on deck; they've got their own servants with them, and seem to be people of consequence."

This conversation was interrupted, but I found my unseen fellow voyagers peculiarly interesting and pursued inquiries in other directions. I saw members of the distinguished travellers' retinue going about their duties, but never obtained a glimpse of Mr. Azraeel nor of any of his green-turbaned companions.

"Who is Mr. Azraeel?" I asked Ahmadeen.

"I cannot say," replied the Egyptian, and abruptly changed the subject.

Some curious aroma of mystery floated about the ship. Ahmadeen conveyed to me the idea that he was concealing something. Then, one night, Mr. Bell invited me to step forward with him.

"Listen," he said.

From somewhere in the fo'c'sle proceeded low chanting.

"Hear it?"

"Yes. What the devil is it?"

"It's the lascars," said Bell. "They have been behaving in a most unusual manner ever since the mysterious Mr. Azraeel joined us. I may be wrong in associating the two things, but I shan't be sorry to see the last of our mysterious passengers."

The next happening on board the Mandalay which I have to record was the attempt to break open the door of Professor Deeping's stateroom. Except when he was actually within, the Professor left his room door religiously locked.

He made light of the affair, but later took me aside and told me a curious story of an apparition which had appeared to him.

"It was a crescent of light," he said, "and it glittered through the darkness there to the left as I lay in my berth."

"A reflection from something on the deck?"

Deeping smiled, uneasily.

"Possibly," he replied; "but it was very sharply defined. Like the blade of a scimitar," he added.

I stared at him, my curiosity keenly aroused. "Does any explanation suggest itself to you?" I said.

"Well," he confessed, "I have a theory, I will admit; but it is rather going back to the Middle Ages. You see, I have lived in the East a lot; perhaps I have assimilated some of their superstitions."

He was oddly reticent, as ever. I felt convinced that he was keeping something back. I could not stifle the impression that the clue to these mysteries lay somewhere around the invisible Mohammedan party.

"Do you know," said Bell to me, one morning, "this trip's giving me the creeps. I believe the damned ship's haunted! Three bells in the middle watch last night, I'll swear I saw some black animal crawling along the deck, in the direction of the forward companion-way."

"Cat?" I suggested.

"Nothing like it," said Mr. Bell. "Mr. Cavanagh, it was some uncanny thing! I'm afraid I can't explain quite what I mean, but it was something I wanted to shoot!"

"Where did it go?"

The chief officer shrugged his shoulders. "Just vanished," he said. "I hope I don't see it again."

At Tilbury the Mohammedan party went ashore in a body. Among them were veiled women. They contrived so to surround a central figure that I entirely failed to get a glimpse of the mysterious Mr. Azraeel. Ahmadeen was standing close by the companion-way, and I had a momentary impression that one of the women slipped something into his hand. Certainly, he started; and his dusky face seemed to pale.

Then a deck steward came out of Deeping's stateroom, carrying the brown bag which the Professor had brought aboard at Port Said. Deeping's voice came:

"Hi, my man! Let me take that bag!"

The bag changed hands. Five minutes later, as I was preparing to go ashore, arose a horrid scream above the berthing clamour. Those passengers yet aboard made in the direction from which the scream had proceeded.

A steward—the one to whom Professor Deeping had spoken—lay writhing at the foot of the stairs leading to the saloon-deck. His right hand had been severed above the wrist!

CHAPTER II
THE GIRL WITH THE VIOLET EYES

During the next day or two my mind constantly reverted to the incidents of the voyage home. I was perfectly convinced that the curtain had been partially raised upon some fantasy in which Professor Deeping figured.

But I had seen no more of Deeping nor had I heard from him, when abruptly I found myself plunged again into the very vortex of his troubled affairs. I was half way through a long article, I remember, upon the mystery of the outrage at the docks. The poor steward whose hand had been severed lay in a precarious condition, but the police had utterly failed to trace the culprit.

I had laid down my pen to relight my pipe (the hour was about ten at night) when a faint sound from the direction of the outside door attracted my attention. Something had been thrust through the letter-box.

"A circular," I thought, when the bell rang loudly, imperatively.

I went to the door. A square envelope lay upon the mat—a curious envelope, pale amethyst in colour. Picking it up, I found it to bear my name—written simply—

"Mr. Cavanagh."

Tearing it open I glanced at the contents. I threw open the door. No one was visible upon the landing, but when I leaned over the banister a white-clad figure was crossing the hall, below.

Without hesitation, hatless, I raced down the stairs. As I crossed the dimly lighted hall and came out into the peaceful twilight of the court, my elusive visitor glided under the archway opposite.

Just where the dark and narrow passage opened on to Fleet Street I overtook her—a girl closely veiled and wrapped in a long coat of white ermine.

"Madam," I said.

She turned affrightedly.

"Please do not detain me!" Her accent was puzzling, but pleasing. She glanced apprehensively about her.

You have seen the moon through a mist?—and known it for what it was in spite of its veiling? So, now, through the cloudy folds of the veil, I saw the stranger's eyes, and knew them for the most beautiful eyes I had ever seen, had ever dreamt of.

"But you must explain the meaning of your note!"

"I cannot! I cannot! Please do not ask me!"

She was breathless from her flight and seemed to be trembling. From behind the cloud her eyes shone brilliantly, mysteriously.

I was sorely puzzled. The whole incident was bizarre—indeed, it had in it something of the uncanny. Yet I could not detain the girl against her will. That she went in apprehension of something, of someone, was evident.

Past the head of the passage surged the noisy realities of Fleet Street. There were men there in quest of news; men who would have given much for such a story as this in which I was becoming entangled. Yet a story more tantalizingly incomplete could not well be imagined.

I knew that I stood upon the margin of an arena wherein strange adversaries warred to a strange end. But a mist was over all. Here, beside me, was one who could disperse the mist—and would not. Her one anxiety seemed to be to escape.

Suddenly she raised her veil; and I looked fully into the only really violet eyes I had ever beheld. Mentally, I started. For the face framed in the snowy fur was the most bewitchingly lovely imaginable. One rebellious lock of wonderful hair swept across the white brow. It was brown hair, with an incomprehensible sheen in the high lights that suggested the heart of a blood-red rose.

"Oh," she cried, "promise me that you will never breathe a word to any one about my visit!"

"I promise willingly," I said; "but can you give me no hint?"

"Honestly, truly, I cannot, dare not, say more! Only promise that you will do as I ask!"

Since I could perceive no alternative—

"I will do so," I replied.

"Thank you—oh, thank you!" she said; and dropping her veil again she walked rapidly away from me, whispering, "I rely upon you. Do not fail me. Good-bye!"

Her conspicuous white figure joined the hurrying throngs upon the pavement beyond. My curiosity brooked no restraint. I hurried to the end of the courtway. She was crossing the road. From the shadows where he had lurked, a man came forward to meet her. A vehicle obstructed the view ere I could confirm my impression; and when it had passed, neither my lovely visitor nor her companion were anywhere in sight.

But, unless some accident of light and shade had deceived me, the man who had waited was Ahmad Ahmadeen!

It seemed that some astral sluice-gate was raised; a dreadful sense of foreboding for the first time flooded my mind. Whilst the girl had stood before me it had been different—the mysterious charm of her personality had swamped all else. But now, the messenger gone, it was the purport of her message which assumed supreme significance.

Written in odd, square handwriting upon the pale amethyst paper, this was the message—

> Prevail upon Professor Deeping to place what he has in the brown case in the porch of his house to-night. If he fails to do so, no power on earth can save him from the Scimitar of Hassan.
> A FRIEND.

CHAPTER III
"HASSAN OF ALEPPO"

Professor Deeping's number was in the telephone directory, therefore, on returning to my room, where there still lingered the faint perfume of my late visitor's presence, I asked for his number. He proved to be at home.

"Strange you should ring me up, Cavanagh," he said; "for I was about to ring you up."

"First," I replied, "listen to the contents of an anonymous letter which I have received."

(I remembered, and only just in time, my promise to the veiled messenger.)

"To me," I added, having read him the note, "it seems to mean nothing. I take it that you understand better than I do."

"I understand very well, Cavanagh!" he replied. "You will recall my story of the scimitar which flashed before me in the darkness of my stateroom on the Mandalay? Well, I have seen it again! I am not an imaginative man: I had always believed myself to possess the scientific mind; but I can no longer doubt that I am the object of a pursuit which commenced in Mecca! The happenings on the steamer prepared me for this, in a degree. When the man lost his hand at Port Said I doubted. I had supposed the days of such things past. The attempt to break into my stateroom even left me still uncertain. But the outrage upon the steward at the docks removed all further doubt. I perceived that the contents of a certain brown leather case were the objective of the crimes."

I listened in growing wonder.

"It was not necessary in order to further the plan of stealing the bag that the hands were severed," resumed the Professor. "In fact, as was rendered evident by the case of the steward, this was a penalty visited upon any one who touched it! You are thinking of my own immunity?"

"I am!"

"This is attributable to two things. Those who sought to recover what I had in the case feared that my death en route might result in its being lost to them for ever. They awaited a suitable opportunity. They had designed to take it at Port Said certainly, I think; but the bag was too large to be readily concealed, and, after the outrage, might have led to the discovery of the culprit. In the second place, they are uncertain of my faith. I have long passed for a true Believer in the East! As a Moslem I visited Mecca—"

"You visited Mecca!"

"I had just returned from the hadj when I joined the Mandalay at Port Said! My death, however, has been determined upon, whether I be Moslem or Christian!"

"Why?"

"Because," came the Professor's harsh voice over the telephone, "of the contents of the brown leather case! I will not divulge to you now the nature of these contents; to know might endanger you. But the case is locked in my safe here, and the key, together with a full statement of the true facts of the matter, is hidden behind the first edition copy of my book 'Assyrian Mythology,' in the smaller bookcase—"

"Why do you tell me all this?" I interrupted.

He laughed harshly.

"The identity of my pursuer has just dawned upon me," he said. "I know that my life is in real danger. I would give up what is demanded of me, but I believe its possession to be my strongest safeguard."

Mystery upon mystery! I seemed to be getting no nearer to the heart of this maze. What in heaven's name did it all mean? Suddenly an idea struck me.

"Is our late fellow passenger, Mr. Ahmadeen, connected with the matter?" I asked.

"In no way," replied Deeping earnestly. "Mr. Ahmadeen is, I believe, a person of some consequence in the Moslem world; but I have nothing to fear from him."

"What steps have you taken to protect yourself?"

Again the short laugh reached my ears.

"I'm afraid long residence in the East has rendered me something of a fatalist, Cavanagh! Beyond keeping my door locked, I have taken no steps whatever. I fear I am quite accessible!"

A while longer we talked; and with every word the conviction was more strongly borne in upon me that some uncanny menace threatened the peace, perhaps the life, of Professor Deeping.

I had hung up the receiver scarce a moment when, acting upon a sudden determination, I called up New Scotland Yard, and asked for Detective-Inspector Bristol, whom I knew well. A few words were sufficient keenly to arouse his curiosity, and he announced his intention of calling upon me immediately. He was in charge of the case of the severed hand.

I made no attempt to resume work in the interval preceding his arrival. I had not long to wait, however, ere Bristol was ringing my bell; and I hurried to the door, only too glad to confide in one so well equipped to analyze my doubts and fears. For Bristol is no ordinary policeman, but a trained observer, who, when I first made his acquaintance, completely upset my ideas upon the mental limitations of the official detective force.

In appearance Bristol suggests an Anglo-Indian officer, and at the time of which I write he had recently returned from Jamaica and his face was as bronzed as a sailor's. One would never take Bristol for a detective. As he seated himself in the armchair, without preamble I plunged into my story. He listened gravely.

"What sort of house is Professor Deeping's?" he asked suddenly.

"I have no idea," I replied, "beyond the fact that it is somewhere in Dulwich."

"May I use your telephone?"

"Certainly."

Very quickly Bristol got into communication with the superintendent of P Division. A brief delay, and the man came to the telephone whose beat included the road wherein Professor Deeping's house was situated.

"Why!" said Bristol, hanging up the receiver after making a number of inquiries, "it's a sort of rambling cottage in extensive grounds. There's only one servant, a manservant, and he sleeps in a detached lodge. If the Professor is really in danger of attack he could not well have chosen a more likely residence for the purpose!"

"What shall you do? What do you make of it all?"

"As I see the case," he said slowly, "it stands something like this: Professor Deeping has..."

The telephone bell began to ring.

I took up the receiver.

"Hullo! Hullo."

"Cavanagh!—is that Cavanagh?"

"Yes! yes! who is that?"

"Deeping! I have rung up the police, and they are sending some one. But I wish..."

His voice trailed off. The sound of a confused and singular uproar came to me.

"Hullo!" I cried. "Hullo!"

A shriek—a deathful, horrifying cry—and a distant babbling alone answered me. There was a crash. Clearly, Deeping had dropped the receiver. I suppose my face blanched.

"What is it?" asked Bristol anxiously.

"God knows what it is!" I said. "Deeping has met with some mishap—"

When, over the wires—

"Hassan of Aleppo!" came a dying whisper. "Hassan ... of Aleppo..."

CHAPTER IV
THE OBLONG BOX

"You had better wait for us," said Bristol to the taxi-man.

"Very good, sir. But I shan't be able to take you further back than the Brixton Garage. You can get another cab there, though."

A clock chimed out—an old-world chime in keeping with the loneliness, the curiously remote loneliness, of the locality. Less than five miles from St. Paul's are spots whereto, with the persistence of Damascus attar, clings the aroma of former days. This iron gateway fronting the old chapel was such a spot.

Just within stood a plain-clothes man, who saluted my companion respectfully.

"Professor Deeping," I began.

The man, with a simple gesture, conveyed the dreadful news.

"Dead! dead!" I cried incredulously.

He glanced at Bristol.

"The most mysterious case I have ever had anything to do with, sir," he said.

The power of speech seemed to desert me. It was unthinkable that Deeping, with whom I had been speaking less than an hour ago, should now be no more; that some malign agency should thus murderously have thrust him into the great borderland.

In that kind of silence which seems to be peopled with whispering spirits we strode forward along the elm avenue. It was very dark where the moon failed to penetrate. The house, low and rambling, came into view, its facade bathed in silver light. Two of the visible windows were illuminated. A sort of loggia ran along one side.

On our left, as we made for this, lay a black ocean of shrubbery. It intruded, raggedly, upon the weed-grown path, for neglect was the keynote of the place.

We entered the cottage, crossed the tiny lobby, and came to the study. A man, evidently Deeping's servant, was sitting in a chair by the door, his head sunken in his hands. He looked up, haggard-faced.

"My God! my God!" he groaned. "He was locked in, gentlemen! He was locked in; and yet something murdered him!"

"What do you mean?" said Bristol. "Where were you?"

"I was away on an errand, sir. When I returned, the police were knocking the door down. He was locked in!"

We passed him, entering the study.

It was a museum-like room, lighted by a lamp on the littered table. At first glance it looked as though some wild thing had run amok there. The disorder was indescribable.

"Touched nothing, of course?" asked Bristol sharply of the officer on duty.

"Nothing, sir. It's just as we found it when we forced the door."

"Why did you force the door?"

"He rung us up at the station and said that something or somebody had got into the house. It was evident the poor gentleman's nerve had broken down, sir. He said he was locked in his study. When we arrived it was all in darkness—but we thought we heard sounds in here."

"What sort of sounds?"

"Something crawling about!"

Bristol turned.

"Key is in the lock on the inside of the door," he said. "Is that where you found it?"

"Yes, sir!"

He looked across to where the brass knob of a safe gleamed dully.

"Safe locked?"

"Yes, sir."

Professor Deeping lay half under the table, a spectacle so ghastly that I shall not attempt to describe it.

"Merciful heavens!" whispered Bristol. "He's nearly decapitated!"

I clutched dizzily at the mantelpiece. It was all so utterly, incredibly horrible. How had Deeping met his death? The windows both were latched and the door had been locked from within!

"You searched for the murderer, of course?" asked Bristol.

"You can see, sir," replied the officer, "that there isn't a spot in the room where a man could hide! And there was nobody in here when we forced the door!"

"Why!" cried my companion suddenly. "The Professor has a chisel in his hand!"

"Yes. I think he must have been trying to prise open that box yonder when he was attacked."

Bristol and I looked, together, at an oblong box which lay upon the floor near the murdered man. It was a kind of small packing case, addressed to Professor Deeping, and evidently had not been opened.

"When did this arrive?" asked Bristol. Lester, the Professor's man, who had entered the room, replied shakily—

"It came by carrier, sir, just before I went out."

"Was he expecting it?"

"I don't think so."

Inspector Bristol and the officer dragged the box fully into the light. It was some three feet long by one foot square, and solidly constructed.

"It is perfectly evident," remarked Bristol, "that the murderer stayed to search for—"

"The key of the safe!"

"Exactly. If the men really heard sounds here, it would appear that the assassin was still searching at that time."

"I assure you," the officer interrupted, "that there was no living thing in the room when we entered."

Bristol and I looked at one another in horrified wonder.

"It's incomprehensible!" he said.

"See if the key is in the place mentioned by the Professor, Mr. Cavanagh, whilst I break the box."

I went to a great, open bookcase, which the frantic searcher seemed to have overlooked. Removing the bulky "Assyrian Mythology," there, behind the volume, lay an envelope, containing a key, and a short letter. Not caring to approach more closely to the table and to that which lay beneath it, I was peering at the small writing, in the semi-gloom by the bookcase, when Bristol cried—

"This box is unopenable by ordinary means! I shall have to smash it!"

At his words, I joined him where he knelt on the floor. Mysteriously, the chest had defied all his efforts.

"There's a pick-axe in the garden," volunteered Lester. "Shall I bring it?"

"Yes."

The man ran off.

"I see the key is safe," said Bristol. "Possibly the letter may throw some light upon all this."

"Let us hope so," I replied. "You might read it."

He took the letter from my hand, stepped up to the table, and by the light of the lamp read as follows—

My Dear Cavanagh,—

> It has now become apparent to me that my life is in imminent danger. You know of the inexplicable outrages which marked my homeward journey, and if this letter come to your hand it will be because these have culminated in my death.
>
> The idea of a pursuing scimitar is not new to me. This phenomenon, which I have now witnessed three times, is fairly easy of explanation, but its significance is singular. It is said to be one of the devices whereby the Hashishin warn those whom they have marked down for destruction, and is called, in the East, "The Scimitar of Hassan."
>
> The Hashishin were the members of a Moslem secret society, founded in 1090 by one Hassan of Khorassan. There is a persistent tradition in parts of the Orient that this sect still flourishes in Assyria, under the rule of a certain Hassan of Aleppo, the Sheikh-al-jebal, or supreme lord of the Hashishin. My careful inquiries, however, at the time that I was preparing matter for my "Assyrian Mythology," failed to discover any trace of such a person or such a group.
>
> I accordingly assumed Hassan to be a myth—a first cousin to the ginn. I was wrong. He exists. And by my supremely rash act I have incurred his vengeance, for Hassan of Aleppo is the self-appointed guardian of the traditions and relics of Mohammed. And I have Stolen one of the holy slippers of the Prophet!

He, with some of his servants, has followed me from Mecca to England. My precautions have enabled me to retain the relic, but you have seen what fate befell all those others who even touched the receptacle containing it.

If I fall a victim to the Hashishin, I am uncertain how you, as my confidant, will fare. Therefore I have locked the slipper in my safe and to you entrust the key. I append particulars of the lock combination; but I warn you—do not open the safe. If their wrath be visited upon you, your possession of the key may prove a safeguard.

Take the copy of "Assyrian Mythology." You will find in it all that I learned respecting the Hashishin. If I am doomed to be assassinated, it may aid you; if not in avenging me, in saving others from my fate. I fear I shall never see you again. A cloud of horror settles upon me like a pall. Do not touch the slipper, nor the case containing it.

EDWARD DEEPING.

"It is almost incredible!" I said hoarsely.

Bristol returned the letter to me without a word, and turning to Lester, who had reentered carrying a heavy pick-axe, he attacked the oblong box with savage energy.

Through the house of death the sound of the blows echoed and rang with a sort of sacrilegious mockery. The box fell to pieces.

"My God! look, sir!"

Lester was the trembling speaker.

The box, I have said, was but three feet long by one foot square, and had clearly defied poor Deeping's efforts to open it. But a crescent-shaped knife, wet with blood, lay within!

CHAPTER V
THE OCCUPANT OF THE BOX

Dimly to my ears came the ceaseless murmur of London. The night now was far advanced, and not a sound disturbed the silence of the court below my windows.

Professor Deeping's "Assyrian Mythology" lay open before me, beside it my notebook. A coal dropped from the fire, and I half started up out of my chair. My nerves were all awry, and I had more than my horrible memories of the murdered man to thank for it. Let me explain what I mean.

When, after assisting, or endeavouring to assist, Bristol at his elaborate inquiries, I had at last returned to my chambers, I had become the victim of a singular delusion—though one common enough in the case of persons whose nerves are overwrought. I had thought myself followed.

During the latter part of my journey I found myself constantly looking from the little window at the rear of the cab. I had an impression that some vehicle was tracking us. Then, when I discharged the man and walked up the narrow passage to the court, it was fear of a skulking form that dodged from shadow to shadow which obsessed me.

Finally, as I entered the hall and mounted the darkened stair, from the first landing I glanced down into the black well beneath. Blazing yellow eyes, I thought, looked up at me!

I will confess that I leapt up the remaining flight of stairs to my door, and, safely within, found myself trembling as if with a palsy.

When I sat down to write (for sleep was an impossible proposition) I placed my revolver upon the table beside me. I cannot say why. It afforded me some sense of protection, I suppose. My conclusions, thus far, amounted to the following—

The apparition of the phantom scimitar was due to the presence of someone who, by means of the moonlight, or of artificial light, cast a reflection of such a weapon as that found in the oblong chest upon the wall of a darkened apartment—as, Deeping's stateroom on the Mandalay, his study, etc.

A group of highly efficient assassins, evidently Moslem fanatics, who might or might not be of the ancient order of the Hashishin, had pursued the stolen slipper to England. They had severed any hand, other than that of a Believer, which had touched the case containing it. (The Coptic porter was a Christian.)

Uncertain, possibly, of Deeping's faith, or fearful of endangering the success of their efforts by an outrage upon him en route, they had refrained from this until his arrival at his house. He had been warned of his impending end by Ahmad Ahmadeen.

Who was Ahmadeen? And who was his beautiful associate? I found myself unable, at present, to answer either of those questions. In order to gain access to Professor Deeping, who so carefully secluded himself, a box had been sent to him by ordinary carrier. (As I sat at my table, Scotland Yard was busy endeavouring to trace the sender.) Respecting this box we had made an extraordinary discovery.

It was of the kind used by Eastern conjurors for what is generally known as "the Box Trick." That is to say, it could only be opened (short of smashing it) from the inside! You will remember what we found within it? Consider this with the new fact, above, and to what conclusion do you come?

Something (it is not possible to speak of someone in connection with so small a box) had been concealed inside, and had killed Professor Deeping whilst he was actually engaged in endeavouring to force it open. This inconceivable creature had then searched the study for the slipper—or for the key of the safe. Interrupted and trapped by the arrival of the police, the creature had returned to the box, re-closed it, and had actually been there when the study was searched!

For a creature so small as the murderous thing in the box to slip out during the confusion, and at some time prior to Bristol's arrival, was no difficult matter. The inspector and I were certain that these were the facts.

But what was this creature?

I turned to the chapter in "Assyrian Mythology"—"The Tradition of the Hashishin."

The legends which the late Professor Deeping had collected relative to this sect of religious murderers were truly extraordinary. Of the cult's extinction at the time of writing he was clearly certain, but he referred to the popular belief, or Moslem legend, that, since Hassan of Khorassan, there had always been a Sheikh-al-jebal, and that a dreadful being known as Hassan of Aleppo was the present holder of the title.

He referred to the fact that De Sacy has shown the word Assassin to be derived from Hashishin, and quoted El-Idrisi to the same end. The Hashishin performed their murderous feats under the influence of hashish, or Indian hemp; and during the state of ecstasy so induced, according to Deeping, they acquired powers almost superhuman. I read how they could scale sheer precipices, pass fearlessly along narrow ledges which would scarce afford foothold for a rat, cast themselves from great heights unscathed, and track one marked for death in such a manner as to remain unseen not only by the victim but by others about him. At this point of my studies I started, in a sudden nervous panic, and laid my hand upon my revolver.

I thought of the eyes which had seemed to look up from the black well of the staircase—I thought of the horrible end of this man whose book lay upon the table ... and I thought I heard a faint sound outside my study door!

The key of Deeping's safe, and his letter to me, lay close by my hand. I slipped them into a drawer and locked it. With every nerve, it seemed, strung up almost to snapping point, I mechanically pursued my reading.

"At the time of the Crusades," wrote Deeping, "there was a story current of this awful Order which I propose to recount. It is one of the most persistent dealing with the Hashishin, and is related to-day of the apparently mythical Hassan of Aleppo. I am disposed to believe that at one time it had a solid foundation, for a similar practice was common in Ancient Egypt and is mentioned by Georg Ebers."

My door began very slowly to open!

Merciful God! What was coming into the room!

So very slowly, so gently, nay, all but imperceptibly, did it move, that had my nerves been less keenly attuned I doubt not I should have remained unaware of the happening. Frozen with horror, I sat and watched. Yet my mental condition was a singular one.

My direct gaze never quitted the door, but in some strange fashion I saw the words of the next paragraph upon the page before me!

"As making peculiarly efficient assassins, when under the influence of the drug, and as being capable of concealing themselves where a normal man could not fail to be detected—"

(At this moment I remembered that my bathroom window was open, and that the waste-pipe passed down the exterior wall.)

"—the Sheikh-al-jebal took young boys of a certain desert tribe, and for eight hours of every day, until their puberty, confined them in a wooden frame—"

What looked like a reed was slowly inserted through the opening between door and doorpost! It was brought gradually around ... until it pointed directly toward me!

I seemed to put forth a mighty mental effort, shaking off the icy hand of fear which held me inactive in my chair. A saving instinct warned me—and I ducked my head.

Something whirred past me and struck the wall behind.

Revolver in hand, I leapt across the room, dashed the door open, and fired blindly—again—and again—and again—down the passage.

And in the brief gleams I saw it!

I cannot call it man, but I saw the thing which, I doubt not, had killed poor Deeping with the crescent-knife and had propelled a poison-dart at me.

It was a tiny dwarf! Neither within nor without a freak exhibition had I seen so small a human being! A kind of supernatural dread gripped me by the throat at sight of it. As it turned with animal activity and bounded into my bathroom, I caught a three-quarter view of the creature's swollen, incredible head—which was nearly as large as that of a normal man!

Never while my mind serves me can I forget that yellow, grinning face and those canine fangs—the tigerish, blazing eyes—set in the great, misshapen head upon the tiny, agile body.

Wildly, I fired again. I hurled myself forward and dashed into the room.

Like nothing so much as a cat, the gleaming body (the dwarf was but scantily clothed) streaked through the open window!

Certain death, I thought, must be his lot upon the stones of the court far below. I ran and looked down, shaking in every limb, my mind filled with a loathing terror unlike anything I had ever known.

Brilliant moonlight flooded the pavement beneath; for twenty yards to left and right every stone was visible.

The court was empty!

Human, homely London moved and wrought intimately about me; but there, at sight of the empty court below, a great loneliness swept down like a mantle—a clammy mantle of the fabric of dread. I stood remote from my fellows, in an evil world peopled with the creatures of Hassan of Aleppo.

Moved by some instinct, as that of a frightened child, I dropped to my knees and buried my face in trembling hands.

CHAPTER VI
THE RING OF THE PROPHET

"There is no doubt," said Mr. Rawson, "that great personal danger attaches to any contact with this relic. It is the first time I have been concerned with anything of the kind."

Mr. Bristol, of Scotland Yard, standing stiffly military by the window, looked across at the gray-haired solicitor. We were all silent for a few moments.

"My late client's wishes," continued Mr. Rawson, "are explicit. His last instructions, evidently written but a short time prior to his death, advise me that the holy slipper of the Prophet is contained in the locked safe at his house in Dulwich. He was clearly of opinion that you, Mr. Cavanagh, would incur risk—great risk—from your possession of the key. Since attempts have been made upon you, murderous attempts, the late Professor Deeping, my unfortunate client, evidently was not in error."

"Mysterious outrages," said Bristol, "have marked the progress of the stolen slipper from Mecca almost to London."

"I understand," interrupted the solicitor, "that a fanatic known as Hassan of Aleppo seeks to restore the relic to its former resting-place."

"That is so."

"Exactly; and it accounts for the Professor's wish that the safe should not be touched by any one but a Believer—and for his instructions that its removal to the Antiquarian Museum and the placing of the slipper within that institution be undertaken by a Moslem or Moslems."

Bristol frowned.

"Any one who has touched the receptacle containing the thing," he said, "has either been mutilated or murdered. I want to apprehend the authors of those outrages, but I fail to see why the slipper should be put on exhibition. Other crimes are sure to follow."

"I can only pursue my instructions," said Mr. Rawson dryly. "They are, that the work be done in such a manner as to expose all concerned to a minimum of risk from these mysterious people; that if possible a Moslem be employed for the purpose; and that Mr. Cavanagh, here, shall always hold the key or keys to the case in the museum containing the slipper. Will you undertake to look for some—Eastern workmen, Mr. Bristol? In the course of your inquiries you may possibly come across such a person."

"I can try," replied Bristol. "Meanwhile, I take it, the safe must remain at Dulwich?"

"Certainly. It should be guarded."

"We are guarding it and shall guard it," Bristol assured him. "I only hope we catch someone trying to get at it!"

Shortly afterward Bristol and I left the office, and, his duties taking him to Scotland Yard, I returned to my chambers to survey the position in which I now found myself. Indeed, it was a strange one enough, showing how great things have small beginnings; for, as a result of a steamer acquaintance I found myself involved in a dark business worthy of the Middle Ages. That Professor Deeping should have stolen one of the holy slippers of Mohammed was no affair of mine, and that an awful being known as Hassan of Aleppo should have pursued it did not properly enter into my concerns; yet now, with a group of Eastern fanatics at large in England, I was become, in a sense, the custodian of the relic. Moreover, I perceived that I had been chosen that I might safeguard myself. What I knew of the matter might imperil me, but whilst I held the key to the reliquary, and held it fast, I might hope to remain immune though I must expect to be subjected to attempts. It would be my affair to come to terms.

Contemplating these things I sat, in a world of dark dreams, unconscious of the comings and goings in the court below, unconscious of the hum which told of busy Fleet Street so near to me. The weather, as is its uncomfortable habit in England, had suddenly grown tropically hot, plunging London into the vapours of an African spring, and the sun was streaming through my open window fully upon the table.

I mopped my clammy forehead, glancing with distaste at the pile of work which lay before me. Then my eyes turned to an open quarto book. It was the late Professor Deeping's "Assyrian Mythology," and embodied the result of his researches into the history of the Hashishin, the religious murderers of whose existence he had been so skeptical. To the Chief of the Order, the terrible Sheikh Hassan of Aleppo, he referred as a "fabled being"; yet it was at the hands of this "fabled being" that he had met his end! How incredible it all seemed. But I knew full well how worthy of credence it was.

Then upon my gloomy musings a sound intruded—the ringing of my door bell. I rose from my chair with a weary sigh, went to the door, and opened it. An aged Oriental stood without. He was tall and straight, had a snow-white beard and clear-cut, handsome features. He wore well-cut European garments and a green turban. As I stood staring he saluted me gravely.

"Mr. Cavanagh?" he asked, speaking in faultless English.

"I am he."

"I learn that the services of a Moslem workman are required."

"Quite correct, sir; but you should apply at the offices of Messrs. Rawson & Rawson, Chancery Lane."

The old man bowed, smiling.

"Many thanks; I understood so much. But, my position being a peculiar one, I wished to speak with you—as a friend of the late Professor."

I hesitated. The old man looked harmless enough, but there was an air of mystery about the matter which put me on my guard.

"You will pardon me," I said, "but the work is scarcely of a kind—"

He raised his thin hand.

"I am not undertaking it myself. I wished to explain to you the conditions under which I could arrange to furnish suitable porters."

His patient explanation disposed me to believe that he was merely some kind of small contractor, and in any event I had nothing to fear from this frail old man.

"Step in, sir," I said, repenting of my brusquerie—and stood aside for him.

He entered, with that Oriental meekness in which there is something majestic. I placed a chair for him in the study, and reseated myself at the table. The old man, who from the first had kept his eyes lowered deferentially, turned to me with a gentle gesture, as if to apologize for opening the conversation.

"From the papers, Mr. Cavanagh," he began, "I have learned of the circumstances attending the death of Professor Deeping. Your papers"—he smiled, and I thought I had never seen a smile of such sweetness—"your papers know all! Now I understand why a Moslem is required, and I understand what is required of him. But remembering that the object of his labours would be to place a holy relic on exhibition for the amusement of unbelievers, can you reasonably expect to obtain the services of one?"

His point of view was fair enough.

"Perhaps not," I replied. "For my own part I should wish to see the slipper back in Mecca, or wherever it came from. But Professor Deeping—"

"Professor Deeping was a thorn in the flesh of the Faithful!"

My visitor's voice was gravely reproachful.

"Nevertheless his wishes must be considered," I said, "and the methods adopted by those who seek to recover the relic are such as to alienate all sympathy."

"You speak of the Hashishin?" asked the old man. "Mr. Cavanagh, in your own faith you have had those who spilled the blood of infidels as freely!"

"My good sir, the existence of such an organization cannot be tolerated today! This survival of the dark ages must be stamped out. However just a cause may be, secret murder is not permissible, as you, a man of culture, a Believer, and"—I glanced at his unusual turban—"a descendant of the Prophet, must admit."

"I can admit nothing against the Guardian of the Tradition, Mr. Cavanagh! The Prophet taught that we should smite the Infidel. I ask you— have you the courage of your convictions?"

"Perhaps; I trust so."

"Then assist me to rid England of what you have called a survival of the dark ages. I will furnish porters to remove and carry the safe, if you will deliver to me the key!"

I sprang to my feet.

"That is madness!" I cried. "In the first place I should be compromising with my conscience, and in the second place I should be defenceless against those who might—"

"I have with me a written promise from one highly placed—one to whose will Hassan of Aleppo bows!"

My mind greatly disturbed, I watched the venerable speaker. I had determined now that he was some religious leader of Islam in England, who had been deputed to approach me; and, let me add, I was sorely tempted to accede to his proposal, for nothing would be gained by any one if the slipper remained for ever at the museum, whereas by conniving at its recovery by those who, after all, were its rightful owners I should be ridding England of a weird and undesirable visitant.

I think I should have agreed, when I remembered that the Hashishin had murdered Professor Deeping and had mutilated others wholly innocent of offence. I looked across at the old man. He had drawn himself up to his great height, and for the first time fully raising the lids, had fixed upon me the piercing gaze of a pair of eagle eyes. I started, for the aspect of this majestic figure was entirely different from that of the old stranger who had stood suppliant before me a moment ago.

"It is impossible," I said. "I can come to no terms with those who shield murderers."

He regarded me fixedly, but did not move.

"Es-selam 'aleykum!" I added ("Peace be on you!") closing the interview in the Eastern manner.

The old man lowered his eyes, and saluted me with graceful gravity.

"Wa-'aleykum!" he said ("And on you!"). I conducted him to the door and closed it upon his exit. In his last salute I had noticed the flashing of a ring which he wore upon his left hand, and he was gone scarce ten seconds ere my heart began to beat furiously. I snatched up "Assyrian Mythology" and with trembling fingers turned to a certain page.

There I read—

Each Sheikh of the Assassins is said to be invested with the "Ring of the Prophet." It bears a green stone, shaped in the form of a scimitar or crescent.

My dreadful suspicion was confirmed. I knew who my visitor had been.

"God in heaven!" I whispered. "It was Hassan of Aleppo!"

CHAPTER VII
FIRST ATTEMPT ON THE SAFE

On the following morning I was awakened by the arrival of Bristol. I hastened to admit him.

"Your visitor of yesterday," he began, "has wasted no time!"

"What has happened?"

He tugged irritably at his moustache. "I don't know!" he replied. "Of course it was no surprise to find that there isn't a Mohammedan who'll lay his little finger on Professor Deeping's safe! There's no doubt in my mind that every lascar at the docks knows Hassan of Aleppo to be in England. Some other arrangement will have to be arrived at, if the thing is ever to be taken to the Antiquarian Museum. Meanwhile we stand to lose it. Last night—"

He accepted a cigarette, and lighted it carefully.

"Last night," he resumed, "a member of P Division was on point duty outside the late Professor's house, and two C.I.D. men were actually in the room where the safe is. Result—someone has put in at least an hour's work on the lock, but it proved too tough a job!"

I stared at him amazedly.

"Someone has been at the lock!" I cried. "But that is impossible, with two men in the room—unless—"

"They were both knocked on the head!"

"Both! But by whom! My God! They are not—"

"Oh, no! It was done artistically. They both came round about four o'clock this morning."

"And who attacked them?"

"They had no idea. Neither of them saw a thing!"

My amazement grew by leaps and bounds. "But, Bristol, one of them must have seen the other succumb!"

"Both did! Their statements tally exactly!"

"I quite fail to follow you."

"That's not surprising. Listen: When I got on the scene about five o'clock, Marden and West, the two C.I.D. men, had quite recovered their senses, though they were badly shaken, and one had a cracked skull. The constable was conscious again, too."

"What! Was he attacked?"

"In exactly the same way! I'll give you Marden's story, as he gave it to me a few minutes after the surgeon had done with him. He said that they were sitting in the study, smoking, and with both windows wide open. It was a fearfully hot night."

"Did they have lights?"

"No. West sat in an armchair near the writing-table; Marden sat by the window next to the door. I had arranged that every hour one of them should go out to the gate and take the constable's report. It was just after Marden had been out at one o'clock that it happened.

"They were sitting as I tell you when Marden thought he heard a curious sort of noise from the gate. West appeared to have heard nothing; but I have no doubt that it was the sound of the constable's fall. West's pipe had gone out, and he struck a match to relight it. As he did so, Marden saw him drop the match, clench both fists, and with eyes glaring in the moonlight and his teeth coming together with a snap, drop from his chair.

"Marden says that he was half up from his seat when something struck him on the back of the head with fearful force. He remembered nothing more until he awoke, with the dawn creeping into the room, and heard West groaning somewhere beside him. They both had badly damaged skulls with great bruises behind the ear. It is instructive to note that their wounds corresponded almost to a fraction of an inch. They had been stunned by someone who thoroughly understood his business, and with some heavy, blunt weapon. A few minutes later came the man to relieve the constable; and the constable was found to have been treated in exactly the same way!"

"But if Marden's account is true—"

"West, as he lost consciousness, saw Marden go in exactly the same way."

"Marden was seated by the open window, but I cannot conjecture how any one can have got at West, who sat by the table!"

"The case of Marden is little less than remarkable; he was some distance from the window. No one could possibly have reached him from outside."

"And the constable?"

"The constable can give us no clue. He was suddenly struck down, as the others were. I examined the safe, of course, but didn't touch it, according to instructions. Someone had been at work on the lock, but it had defied their efforts. I'm fully expecting though that they'll be back to-night, with different tools!"

"The place is watched during the day, of course?"

"Of course. But it's unlikely that anything will be attempted in daylight. Tonight I am going down myself."

"Could you arrange that I join you?"

"I could, but you can see the danger for yourself?"

"It is extraordinarily mysterious."

"Mr. Cavanagh, it's uncanny!" said Bristol. "I can understand that one of these Hashishin could easily have got up behind the man on duty out in the open. I know, and so do you, that they're past masters of that kind of thing; but unless they possess the power to render themselves invisible, it's not evident how they can have got behind West whilst he sat at the table, with Marden actually watching him!"

"We must lay a trap for them to-night."

"Rely upon me to do so. My only fear is that they may anticipate it and change their tactics. Hassan of Aleppo apparently knows as much of our plans as we do ourselves."

Inspector Bristol, though a man of considerable culture, clearly was infected with a species of supernatural dread.

CHAPTER VIII
THE VIOLET EYES AGAIN

At four o'clock in the afternoon I had heard nothing further from Bristol, but I did not doubt that he would advise me of his arrangements in good time. I sought by hard work to forget for a time the extraordinary business of the stolen slipper; but it persistently intruded upon my mind. Particularly, my thoughts turned to the night of Professor Deeping's murder, and to the bewitchingly pretty woman who had warned me of the impending tragedy. She had bound me to secrecy—a secrecy which had proved irksome, for it had since appeared to me that she must have been an accomplice of Hassan of Aleppo. At the time I had been at a loss to define her peculiar accent, now it seemed evidently enough to have been Oriental.

I threw down my pen in despair, for work was impossible, went downstairs, and walked out under the arch into Fleet Street. Quite mechanically I turned to the left, and, still engaged with idle conjectures, strolled along westward.

Passing the entrance to one of the big hotels, I was abruptly recalled to the realities—by a woman's voice.

"Wait for me here," came musically to my ears.

I stopped, and turned. A woman who had just quitted a taxi-cab was entering the hotel. The day was hot and thunderously oppressive, and this woman with the musical voice wore a delicate costume of flimsiest white. A few steps upward she paused and glanced back. I had a view of a Greek profile, and for one magnetic instant looked into eyes of the deepest and most wonderful violet.

Then, shaking off inaction, I ran up the steps and overtook the lady in white as a porter swung open the door to admit her. We entered together.

"Madame," I said in a low tone, "I must detain you for a moment. There is something I have to ask."

She turned, exhibiting the most perfect composure, lowered her lashes and raised them again, the gaze of the violet eyes sweeping me from head to foot with a sort of frigid scorn.

"I fear you have made a mistake, sir. We have never met before!"

Her voice betrayed no trace of any foreign accent!

"But," I began—and paused.

I felt myself flush; for this encounter in the foyer of an hotel, with many curious onlookers, was like to prove embarrassing if my beautiful acquaintance persisted in her attitude. I fully realized what construction would be put upon my presence there, and foresaw that forcible and ignominious ejection must be my lot if I failed to establish my right to address her.

She turned away, and crossed in the direction of the staircase. A sunbeam sought out a lock of hair that strayed across her brow, and kissed it to a sudden glow like that which lurks in the heart of a blush rose.

That wonderful sheen, which I had never met with elsewhere in nature, but which no artifice could lend, served to remove my last frail doubt which had survived the evidence of the violet eyes. I had been deceived by no strange resemblance; this was indeed the woman who had been the harbinger of Professor Deeping's death. In three strides I was beside her again. Curious glances were set upon me, and I saw a servant evidently contemplating approach; but I ignored all save my own fixed purpose.

"You must listen to what I have to say!" I whispered. "If you decline, I shall have no alternative but to call in the detective who holds a warrant for your arrest!"

She stood quite still, watching me coolly. "I suppose you would wish to avoid a scene?" I added.

"You have already made me the object of much undesirable attention," she replied scornfully. "I do not need your assurance that you would disgrace me utterly! You are talking nonsense, as you must be aware—unless you are insane. But if your object be to force your acquaintance upon me, your methods are novel, and, under the circumstances, effective. Come, sir, you may talk to me—for three minutes!"

The musical voice had lost nothing of its imperiousness, but for one instant the lips parted, affording a fleeting glimpse of pearl beyond the coral.

Her sudden change of front was bewildering. Now, she entered the lift and I followed her. As we ascended side by side I found it impossible to believe that this dainty white figure was that of an associate of the Hashishin, that of a creature of the terrible Hassan of Aleppo. Yet that she was the same girl who, a few days after my return from the East, had shown herself conversant with the plans of the murderous fanatics was beyond doubt. Her accent on that occasion clearly had been assumed, with what object I could not imagine. Then, as we quitted the lift and entered a cosy lounge, my companion seated herself upon a Chesterfield, signing to me to sit beside her.

As I did so she lay back smiling, and regarding me from beneath her black lashes. Thus, half veiled, her great violet eyes were most wonderful.

"Now, sir," she said softly, "explain yourself."

"Then you persist in pretending that we have not met before?"

"There is no occasion for pretence," she replied lightly; and I found myself comparing her voice with her figure, her figure with her face, and vainly endeavouring to compute her age. Frankly, she was bewildering—this lovely girl who seemed so wholly a woman of the world.

"This fencing is useless."

"It is quite useless! Come, I know New York, London, and I know Paris, Vienna, Budapest. Therefore I know mankind! You thought I was pretty, I suppose? I may be; others have thought so. And you thought you would like to make my acquaintance without troubling about the usual formalities? You adopted a singularly brutal method of achieving your object, but I love such insolence in a man. Therefore I forgave you. What have you to say to me?"

I perceive that I had to deal with a bold adventuress, with a consummate actress, who, finding herself in a dangerous situation, had adopted this daring line of defence, and now by her personal charm sought to lure me from my purpose.

But with the scimitar of Hassan of Aleppo stretched over me, with the dangers of the night before me, I was in no mood for a veiled duel of words, for an interchange of glances in thrust and parry, however delightful such warfare might have been with so pretty an adversary.

For a long time I looked sternly into her eyes; but their violet mystery defied, whilst her red-lipped smile taunted me.

"Unfortunately," I said, with slow emphasis, "you are protected by my promise, made on the occasion of our previous meeting. But murder has been done, so that honour scarcely demands that I respect my promise further—"

She raised her eyebrows slightly.

"Surely that depends upon the quality of the honour!" she said.

"I believe you to be a member of a murderous organization, and unless you can convince me that I am wrong, I shall act accordingly."

At that she leaned toward me, laying her hand on my arm.

"Please do not be so cruel," she whispered, "as to drag me into a matter with which truly I have no concern. Believe me, you are utterly mistaken. Wait one moment, and I will prove it."

She rose, and before I could make move to detain her, quitted the room; but the door scarcely had closed ere I was afoot. The corridor beyond was empty. I ran on. The lift had just descended. A dark man whom I recognized stood near the closed gate.

"Quick!" I said, "I am Cavanagh of the Report! Did you see a lady enter the lift?"

"I did, Mr. Cavanagh," answered the hotel detective; for this was he.

In such a giant inn as this I knew full well that one could come and go almost with impunity, though one had no right to the hospitality of the establishment; and it was with a premonition respecting what his answer would be, that I asked the man—

"Is she staying here?"

"She is not. I have never seen her before!"

The girl with the violet eyes had escaped, taking all her secrets with her!

CHAPTER IX
SECOND ATTEMPT ON THE SAFE

"You see," said Bristol, "the Hashishin must know that the safe won't remain here unopened much longer. They will therefore probably make another attempt to-night."

"It seems likely," I replied; and was silent. Outside the open windows whispered the shrubbery, as a soft breeze stole through the bushes. Beyond, the moon made play in the dim avenue. From the old chapel hard by the sweet-toned bell proclaimed midnight. Our vigil was begun. In this room it was that Professor Deeping had met death at the hands of the murderous Easterns; here it was that Marden and West had mysteriously been struck down the night before.

To-night was every whit as hot, and Bristol and I had the windows widely opened. My companion was seated where the detective, Marden, had sat, in a chair near the westerly window, and I lay back in the armchair that had been occupied by West.

I may repeat here that the house of the late Professor Deeping was more properly a cottage, surrounded by a fairly large piece of ground, for the most part run wild. The room used as a study was on the ground floor, and had windows on the west and on the south. Those on the west (French windows) opened on a loggia; those on the south opened right into the dense tangle of a neglected shrubbery. The place possessed an oppressive atmosphere of loneliness, for which in some measure its history may have been responsible.

The silence, seemingly intensified by each whisper that sped through the elms and crept about the shrubbery, grew to such a stillness that I told myself I had experienced nothing like it since crossing with a caravan I had slept in the desert. Yet noisy, whirling London was within gunshot of us; and this, though hard enough to believe, was a reflection oddly comforting. Only one train of thought was possible, and this I pursued at random.

By what means were Marden and West struck down? In thus exposing ourselves, in order that we might trap the author or authors of the outrage, did we act wisely?

"Bristol," I said suddenly, "it was someone who came through the open window."

"No one," he replied, "came through the windows. West saw absolutely nothing. But if any one comes that way to-night, we have him!"

"West may have seen nothing; but how else could any one enter?"

Bristol offered no reply; and I plunged again into a maze of speculation.

Powerful mantraps were set in such a way that any one or anything, ignorant of their positions, coming up to the windows must unavoidably be snared. These had been placed in position with much secrecy after dusk, and the man on duty at the gate stood with his back to the wall. No one could approach him except from the front. My thoughts took a new turn.

Was the girl with the violet eyes an ally of the Hashishin? Thus far, although she so palpably had tricked me, I had found myself unable to speak of her to Bristol; for the idea had entered my mind that she might have learned of the plan to murder Deeping without directly being implicated. Now came yet another explanation. The publicity given to that sensational case might have interested some third party in the fate of the stolen slipper! Could it be that others, in no way connected with the dreadful Hassan of Aleppo, were in quest of the slipper?

Scotland Yard had taken care to ensure that the general public be kept in ignorance of the existence of such an organization as the Hashishin, but I must assume that this hypothetical third party were well aware that they had Hassan, as well as the authorities, to count with. Granting the existence of such a party, my beautiful acquaintance might be classified as one of its members. I spoke again.

"Bristol," I said, "has it occurred to you that there may be others, as well as Hassan of Aleppo, seeking to gain possession of the sacred slipper?"

"It has not," he replied. "In the strictest sense of the expression, they would be out for trouble! What gave you the idea?"

"I hardly know," I returned evasively, for even now I was loath to betray the mysterious girl with the wonderful eyes.

The chapel bell sounding the half-hour, Bristol rose with a sigh that might have been one of relief, and went out to take the report of the man on duty at the gate. As his footsteps died away along the elm avenue, it came to me how, in the darkness about, menace lurked; and I felt myself succumbing to the greatest dread experienced by man—the dread of the unknown.

All that I knew of the weird group of fanatics—survivals of a dim and evil past—who must now be watching this cottage as bloodlustful devotees watch a shrine violated, burst upon my mind. I peopled the still blackness with lurking assassins, armed with the murderous knowledge of by-gone centuries, armed with invisible weapons which struck down from afar, supernaturally.

I glanced toward the corner of the room where the safe stood, reliquary of a worthless thing for which much blood had been spilled.

Then sounded footsteps along the avenue, and my fear whispered that they were not those of Bristol but of one who had murdered him, and who came guilefully, to murder me!

I snatched the revolver from my pocket and crossed the darkened room. Just to the right of one of the French windows I stood looking out across the loggia to the end of the avenue. The night was a bright one, and the room was flooded with a reflected mystic light, but outside the moon paved the avenue with pearl, and through the trees I saw a figure approaching.

Was it Bristol? It had his build, it had his gait; but my fears remained. Then the figure crossed the patch of shrubbery and stepped on to the loggia.

"Mr. Cavanagh!"

I laughed dryly at my own cowardice, but my heart was still beating abnormally.

"Here I am, Bristol, in a ghastly funk!"

"I don't wonder! They may be on us any time now. All's well at the gate, but Morris says he heard, or thought he heard something at the side of the chapel opposite, a while ago."

"Wind in the bushes?"

"It may have been; but he says there was no breeze at the time."

We resumed our seats.

"Bristol," I said, "now that the danger grows imminent, doesn't it seem to you foolhardy for us thus to expose ourselves?"

"Perhaps it is," he agreed; "but how otherwise are we likely to learn what happened to Marden and West?"

"The enemy may adopt different measures to-night."

"I think not. Our dispositions are the same, and I credit them with cunning enough to know it. At the same time I credit ourselves with having kept the existence of the steel traps completely secret. They will assume (so I've reasoned) that we intend to rely entirely upon our superior vigilance, therefore they will try the same game as last night."

Silence fell.

The moon rays, creeping around from the right of the avenue, crossing the shrubbery and encroaching upon the low wall of the loggia, now flooded its floor. Against the silvern light, Bristol appeared to me in black silhouette. The breeze, too, seemed now to blow from a slightly different direction. It came through the windows on my right, beyond which lay the unkempt bushes which extended on that side to the wall of the grounds.

So we sat, until the moonlight poured fully in upon Bristol's back. So we sat when the clock chimed the hour of one.

Bristol arose and once more went out to the gate. He had arranged to visit Morris's post every half-hour. Again I experienced the nervous dread that he would be attacked in the avenue; but again he returned unscathed.

"All's well," he said.

But from his tones I knew that he had not forgotten that it was at this hour Marden and West had suffered mysterious attack.

Neither of us, I think, was disposed to talk. We both were unwilling to break the silence, wherein, with all our ears, we listened for the slightest disturbance.

And now my attention turned anew to the course of the slowly creeping moon rays. In my mind an idea was struggling for definition. There was something significant in the lunar lighting of the room. Why, I asked myself, had the attack been made at one o'clock? Did the time signify anything? If so, what? I looked toward Bristol.

His figure, the chair upon which he sat, were sharply outlined by the cold light. The wall behind me, and to my left, was illuminated brilliantly; but no light fell directly upon me.

The idea was taking shape. From the loggia and the avenue Bristol, I reasoned, must be clearly visible. From the shrubbery on the south, through the other windows could I be seen? Yes, silhouetted against the moonlight!

A faint sound, quite indescribable, came to my ears from somewhere outside-beyond.

"My God!" whispered Bristol. "Did you hear it?"

"Yes! What?"

"It must have been Morris!—"

Bristol was half standing, one hand upon the arm of the chair, the other concealed, but grasping his revolver as I well knew. I, too, had my revolver in my hand, and as I twisted in my seat, preparatory to rising, in sheer nervousness I dropped the weapon upon the carpet.

With an exclamation of dismay, I stooped quickly to recover it.

As I did so something whistled past my ear, so closely as almost to touch it—and struck with a dull thud upon the wall beyond!

"Bristol!" I whispered.

But as I raised my eyes to him he seemed to crumple up, and fell loosely forward into the patch of moonlight spread upon the floor! "God in heaven!" I said aloud.

In a cold sweat of fear I crouched there, for it had become evident to me that, as I bent, I was entirely in shadow.

There was a rustling in the bushes on the left; but before I could turn in that direction, my attention was claimed elsewhere. Over into the loggia leapt an almost naked brown figure!

It was that of a small but strongly built man, who carried a short, exceedingly thick bamboo rod in his hand. My fear was too great to admit of my accurately observing anything at that time, but I noticed that some kind of leather thong or loop was attached to the end of the squat cane.

The panic fear of the supernatural was strongly upon me, and I was unable to realize that this Eastern apparition was a creature of flesh and blood. With my nerves strung up to snapping point, I crouched watching him. He entered the room, bending over the body of Bristol.

A hot breath fanned my cheek!

At that my overwrought nerves betrayed me. I uttered a stifled cry, looking upward ... and into a pair of gleaming eyes which looked down into mine!

A second brown man (who must have entered by one of the windows overlooking the shrubbery) was bending over me!

Scarce knowing what I did, I raised my revolver and blazed straight into the dimly-seen face. Down upon me silently dropped a naked body, and something warm came flowing over my hand. But, knowing my foes to be of flesh and blood, feeling myself at handgrips now with a palpable enemy, I threw off the body, leapt up and fired, though blindly, at the flying shape that flashed across the loggia—and was lost in the shadow pools under the elms.

Upon the din of my shooting fell silence like a cloak. A moment I listened, tense, still; then I turned to the table and lighted the lamp.

In its light I saw Bristol lying like a dead man. Close beside him was a big and heavy lump of clay. It had been shaped as a ball, but now it was flattened out curiously. Bending over my unfortunate companion and learning that, though unconscious, he lived, I learnt, too, how the Hashishin contrived to strike men insensible without approaching them; I learnt that the one whom I had shot, who lay in his blood almost on the spot where Professor Deeping once had lain, was an expert slinger.

The contrivance which he carried, as did the other who had escaped, was a sling, of the ancient Persian type. In place of stones, heavy lumps of clay were used, which operated much the same as a sand-bag, whilst enabling the operator to work from a considerable distance.

Hidden, over by the ancient chapel it might be, one of this evil twain had struck down Morris, the constable; from the shelter of the trees, from many yards away, they had shot their singular missiles through the open windows at Bristol and myself. Bristol had succumbed, and now, with a redness showing through his close-cut hair immediately behind the right ear, lay wholly unconscious at my feet.

It had been a divine accident which had caused me to drop my revolver, and, stooping to recover it, unknowingly to frustrate the design of the second slinger upon myself. The light of the lamp fell upon the face of the dead Hashishin. He lay forward upon his hands, crouching almost, but with his face, his dreadful, featureless face, twisted up at me from under his left shoulder.

God knows he deserved his end; but that mutilated face is often grinning, bloodily, in my dreams.

And then as I stood, between that horrid exultation which is born of killing and the panic which threatened me out of the darkness, I saw something advancing ... slowly ... slowly ... from the elmen shades toward the loggia.

It was a shape—it was a shadow. Silent it came—on—and on. Where the dusk lay deepest it paused, undefined; for I could give it no name of man or spirit. But a horror seemed to proceed from it as light from a lamp.

I groped about the table near to me, never taking my eyes from that sinister form outside. As my fingers closed upon the telephone, distant voices and the sound of running footsteps (of those who had heard the shots) came welcome to my ears.

The form stirred, seeming to raise phantom arms in execration, and a stray moonbeam pierced the darkness shrouding it. For a fleeting instant something flashed venomously.

The sounds grew nearer. I could tell that the newcomers had found Morris lying at the gate. Yet still I stood, frozen with uncanny fear, and watching—watching the spot to which that stray beam had pierced; the spot where I had seen the moon gleam upon the ring of the Prophet!

CHAPTER X
AT THE BRITISH ANTIQUARIAN MUSEUM

A little group of interested spectators stood at the head of the square glass case in the centre of the lofty apartment in the British Antiquarian Museum known as the Burton Room (by reason of the fact that a fine painting of Sir Richard Burton faces you as you enter). A few other people looked on curiously from the lower end of the case. It contained but one exhibit—a dirty and dilapidated markoob—or slipper of morocco leather that had once been red.

"Our latest acquisition, gentlemen," said Mr. Mostyn, the curator, speaking in a low tone to the distinguished Oriental scholars around him. "It has been left to the Institution by the late Professor Deeping. He describes it in a document furnished by his solicitor as one of the slippers worn by the Prophet Mohammed, but gives us no further particulars. I myself cannot quite place the relic."

"Nor I," interrupted one of the group. "It is not mentioned by any of the Arabian historians to my knowledge—that is, if it comes from Mecca, as I understand it does."

"I cannot possibly assert that it comes from Mecca, Dr. Nicholson," Mostyn replied. "The Professor may have taken it from Al-Madinah—perhaps from the mysterious inner passage of the baldaquin where the treasures of the place lie. But I can assure you that what little we do know of its history is sufficiently unsavoury."

I fancied that the curator's tired cultured voice faltered as he spoke; and now, without apparent reason, he moved a step to the right and glanced oddly along the room. I followed the direction of his glance, and saw a tall man in conventional morning dress, irreproachable in every detail, whose head was instantly bent upon his catalogue. But before his eyes fell I knew that their long almond shape, as well as the peculiar burnt pallor of his countenance, were undoubtedly those of an Oriental.

"There have been mysterious outrages committed, I believe, upon many of those who have come in contact with the slipper?" asked one of the savants.

"Exactly. Professor Deeping was undoubtedly among the victims. His instructions were explicit that the relic should be brought here by a Moslem, but for a long time we failed to discover any Moslem who would undertake the task; and, as you are aware, while the slipper remained at the Professor's house attempts were made to steal it."

He ceased uneasily, and glanced at the tall Eastern figure. It had edged a little nearer; the head was still bowed and the fine yellow waxen fingers of the hand from which he had removed his glove fumbled with the catalogue's leaves. It may well have been that in those days I read menace in every eye, yet I felt assured that the yellow visitor was eavesdropping—was malignantly attentive to the conversation.

The curator spoke lower than ever now; no one beyond the circle could possibly hear him as he proceeded—

"We discovered an Alexandrian Greek who, for personal reasons, not unconnected with matrimony, had turned Moslem! He carried the slipper here, strongly escorted, and placed it where you now see it. No other hand has touched it." (The speaker's voice was raised ever so slightly.) "You will note that there is a rail around the case, to prevent visitors from touching even the glass."

"Ah," said Dr. Nicholson quizzically, "And has anything untoward happened to our Graeco-Moslem friend?"

"Perhaps Inspector Bristol can tell," replied the curator.

The straight, military figure of the well-known Scotland Yard man was conspicuous among the group of distinguished—and mostly round-shouldered—scholars.

"Sorry, gentlemen," he said, smiling, "but Mr. Acepulos has vanished from his tobacco shop in Soho. I am not apprehensive that he had been kidnapped or anything of that kind. I think rather that the date of his disappearance tallies with that on which he cashed his cheque for service rendered! His present wife is getting most unbeautifully fat, too."

"What precautions," someone asked, "are being taken to guard the slipper?"

"Well," Mostyn answered, "though we have only the bare word of the late Professor Deeping that the slipper was actually worn by Mohammed, it has certainly an enormous value according to Moslem ideas. There can be no doubt that a group of fanatics known as Hashishin are in London engaged in an extraordinary endeavour to recover it."

Mostyn's voice sank to an impressive whisper. My gaze sought again the tall Eastern visitor and was held fascinated by the baffled straining in those velvet eyes. But the lids fell as I looked; and the effect was that of a fire suddenly extinguished. I determined to draw Bristol's attention to the man.

"Accordingly," Mostyn continued, "we have placed it in this room, from which I fancy it would puzzle the most accomplished thief to remove it."

The party, myself included, stared about the place, as he went on to explain—

"We have four large windows here; as you see. The Burton Room occupies the end of a wing; there is only one door; it communicates with the next room, which in turn opens into the main building by another door on the landing. We are on the first floor; these two east windows afford a view of the lawn before the main entrance; those two west ones face Orpington Square; all are heavily barred as you see. During the day there is a man always on duty in these two rooms. At night that communicating door is locked. Short of erecting a ladder in full view either of the Square or of Great Orchard Street, filing through four iron bars and breaking the window and the case, I fail to see how anybody can get at the slipper here."

"If a duplicate key to the safe—" another voice struck in; I knew it afterward for that of Professor Rhys-Jenkyns.

"Impossible to procure one, Professor," cried Mostyn, his eyes sparkling with an almost boyish interest. "Mr. Cavanagh here holds the keys of the case, under the will of the late Professor Deeping. They are of foreign workmanship and more than a little complicated."

The eyes of the savants were turned now in my direction.

"I suppose you have them in a place of safety?" said Dr. Nicholson.

"They are at my bankers," I replied.

"Then I venture to predict," said the celebrated Orientalist, "that the slipper of the Prophet will rest here undisturbed."

He linked his arm into that of a brother scholar and the little group straggled away, Mostyn accompanying them to the main entrance.

But I saw Inspector Bristol scratching his chin; he looked very much as if he doubted the accuracy of the doctor's prediction. He had already had some experience of the implacable devotion of the Moslem group to this treasure of the Faithful.

"The real danger begins," I suggested to him, "when the general public is admitted—after to-day, is it not?"

"Yes. All to-day's people are specially invited, or are using special invitation cards," he replied. "The people who received them often give their tickets away to those who will be likely really to appreciate the opportunity."

I looked around for the tall Oriental. He seemed to have vanished, and for some reason I hesitated to speak of him to Bristol; for my gaze fell upon an excessively thin, keen-faced man whose curiously wide-open eyes met mine smilingly, whose gray suit spoke Stein-Bloch, whose felt was a Boss raw-edge unmistakably of a kind that only Philadelphia can produce. At the height of the season such visitors are not rare, but this one had an odd personality, and moreover his keen gaze was raking the place from ceiling to floor.

Where had I met him before? To the best of my recollection I had never set eyes upon the man prior to that moment; and since he was so palpably an American I had no reason for assuming him to be associated with the Hashishin. But I remembered—indeed, I could never forget—how, in the recent past, I had met with an apparent associate of the Moslems as evidently European as this curiously alert visitor was American. Moreover ... there was something tauntingly familiar, yet elusive, about that gaunt face.

Was it not upon the eve of the death of Professor Deeping that the girl with the violet eyes had first intruded her fascinating personality into my tangled affairs? Patently, she had then been seeking the holy slipper, and by craft had endeavoured to bend me to her will. Then had I not encountered her again, meeting the glance of her unforgettable violet eyes outside a Strand hotel? The encounter had presaged a further attempt upon the slipper! Certainly she acted on behalf of someone interested in it; and since neither Bristol nor I could conceive of any one seeking to possess the bloodstained thing except the mysterious leader of the Hashishin—Hassan of Aleppo—as a creature of that awful fanatic being I had written her down.

Why, then, if the mysterious Eastern employed a European girl, should he not also employ an American man? It might well be that the relic, in entering the doors of the impregnable Antiquarian Museum, had passed where the diabolical arts of the Hashishin had no power to reach it—where the beauty of Western women and the craft of Eastern man were equally useless weapons. Perhaps Hassan's campaign was entering upon a new phase.

Was it a shirking of plain duty on my part that wish—that ever-present hope—that the murderous company of fanatics who had pursued the stolen slipper from its ancient resting-place to London, should succeed in recovering it? I leave you to judge.

The crescent of Islam fades to-day and grows pale, but there are yet fierce Believers, alust for the blood of the infidel. In such as these a faith dies the death of an adder, and is more venomous in its death-throes than in the full pulse of life. The ghastly indiscretion of Professor Deeping, in rifling a Moslem Sacristy, had led to the mutilation of many who, unwittingly, had touched the looted relic, had brought about his own end, had established a league of fantastic assassins in the heart of the metropolis.

Only once had I seen the venerable Hassan of Aleppo—a stately, gentle old man; but I knew that the velvet eyes could blaze into a passionate fury that seemed to scorch whom it fell upon. I knew that the saintly Hassan was Sheikh of the Hashishin. And familiarity with that dreadful organization had by no means bred contempt. I was the holder of the key, and my fear of the fanatics grew like a magic mango, darkened the sunlight of each day, and filled the night with indefinable dread.

You, who have not read poor Deeping's "Assyrian Mythology", cannot picture a creature with a huge, distorted head, and a tiny, dwarfed body—a thing inhuman, yet human—a man stunted and malformed by the cruel arts of brother men—a thing obnoxious to life, with but one passion, the passion to kill. You cannot conceive of the years of agony spent by that creature strapped to a wooden frame—in order to prevent his growth! You cannot conceive of his fierce hatred of all humanity, inflamed to madness by the Eastern drug, hashish, and directed against the enemies of Islam—the holders of the slipper—by the wonderful power of Hassan of Aleppo.

But I had not only read of such beings, I had encountered one!

And he was but one of the many instruments of the Hashishin. Perhaps the girl with the violet eyes was another. What else to be dreaded Hassan might hold in store for us I could not conjecture.

Do you wonder that I feared? Do you wonder that I hoped (I confess it), hoped that the slipper might be recovered without further bloodshed?

CHAPTER XI
THE HOLE IN THE BLIND

I stepped over to the door, where a constable stood on duty.

"You observed a tall Eastern gentleman in the room a while ago, officer?"

"I did, sir."

"How long is he gone?"

The man started and began to peer about anxiously.

"That's a funny thing, sir," he said. "I was keeping my eyes specially upon him. I noticed him hovering around while Mr. Mostyn was speaking; but although I could have sworn he hadn't passed out, he's gone!"

"You didn't notice his departure, then?"

"I'm sorry to say I didn't, sir."

The man clearly was perplexed, but I found small matter for wonder in the episode. I had more than suspected the stranger to be a spy of Hassan's, and members of that strange company were elusive as will-o'-the-wisps.

Bristol, at the far end of the room, was signalling to me. I walked back and joined him.

"Come over here," he said, in a low voice, "and pretend to examine these things."

He glanced significantly to his left. Following the glance, my eyes fell upon the lean American; he was peering into the receptacle which held the holy slipper.

Bristol led me across the room, and we both faced the wall and bent over a glass case. Some yellow newspaper cuttings describing its contents hung above it, and these we pretended to read.

"Did you notice that man I glanced at?"

"Yes."

"Well, that's Earl Dexter, the first crook in America! Ssh! Only goes in on very big things. We had word at the Yard he was in town; but we can't touch him—we can only keep our eyes on him. He usually travels openly and in his own name, but this time he seems to have slipped over quietly. He always dresses the same and has just given me 'good day!' They call him The Stetson Man. We heard this morning that he had booked two first-class sailings in the Oceanic, leaving for New York three weeks hence. Now, Mr. Cavanagh, what is his game?"

"It has occurred to me before, Bristol," I replied, "and you may remember that I mentioned the idea to you, that there might be a third party interested in the slipper. Why shouldn't Earl Dexter be that third party?"

"Because he isn't a fool," rapped Bristol shortly. "Earl Dexter isn't a man to gather up trouble for himself. More likely if his visit has anything really to do with the slipper he's retained by Hassan and Company. Museum-breaking may be a bit out of the line of Hashishin!"

This latter suggestion dovetailed with my own ideas, and oddly enough there was something positively wholesome in the notion of the straightforward crookedness of a mere swell cracksman.

Then happened a singular thing, and one that effectually concluded our whispered colloquy. From the top end of the room, beyond the case containing the slipper, one of the yellow blinds came down with a run.

Bristol turned in a flash. It was not a remarkable accident, and might portend no more than a loose cord; but when, having walked rapidly up the room, we stood before the lowered blind, it appeared that this was no accident at all.

Some four feet from the bottom of the blind (or five feet from the floor) a piece of linen a foot square had been neatly slashed out!

I glanced around the room. Several fashionably dressed visitors were looking idly in our direction, but I could fasten upon no one of them as a likely perpetrator.

Bristol stared at me in perplexity.

"Who on earth did it," he muttered, "and what the blazes for?"

CHAPTER XII
THE HASHISHIN WATCH

"The American gentleman has just gone out, sir," said the sergeant at the door.

I nodded grimly and raced down the steps. Despite my half-formed desire that the slipper should be recovered by those to whom properly it belonged, I experienced at times a curious interest in its welfare. I cannot explain this. Across the hall in front of me I saw Earl Dexter passing out of the Museum. I followed him through into Kingsway and thence to Fleet Street. He sauntered easily along, a nonchalant gray figure. I had begun to think that he was bound for his hotel and that I was wasting my time when he turned sharply into quiet Salisbury Square; it was almost deserted.

My heart leapt into my mouth with a presentiment of what was coming as I saw an elegant and beautifully dressed woman sauntering along in front of us on the far side.

Was it that I detected something familiar in her carriage, in the poise of her head—something that reminded me of former unforgettable encounters; encounters which without exception had presaged attempts upon the slipper of the Prophet? Or was it that I recollected how Dexter had booked two passages to America? I cannot say, but I felt my heart leap; I knew beyond any possibility of doubt that this meeting in Salisbury Square marked the opening of a new chapter in the history of the slipper.

Dexter slipped his arm within that of the girl in front of him and they paced slowly forward in earnest conversation. I suppose my action was very amateurish and very poor detective work; but regardless of discovery I crossed the road and passed close by the pair.

I am certain that Dexter was speaking as I came up, but, well out of earshot, his voice was suddenly arrested. His companion turned and looked at me.

I was prepared for it, yet was thrilled electrically by the flashing glance of the violet eyes—for it was she—the beautiful harbinger of calamities!

My brain was in a whirl; complication piled itself upon complication; yet in the heart of all this bewilderment I thought I could detect the key of the labyrinth, but at the time my ideas were in disorder, for the violet eyes were not lowered but fixed upon me in cold scorn.

I knew myself helpless, and bending my head with conscious embarrassment I passed on hurriedly.

I had work to do in plenty, but I could not apply my mind to it; and now, although the obvious and sensible thing was to go about my business, I wandered on aimlessly, my brain employed with a hundred idle conjectures and the query, "Where have I seen The Stetson Man?" seeming to beat, like a tattoo, in my brain. There was something magnetic about the accursed slipper, for without knowing by what route I had arrived there, I found myself in Great Orchard Street and close under the walls of the British Antiquarian Museum. Then I was effectually aroused from my reverie.

Two men, both tall, stood in the shadow of a doorway on the Opposite side of the street, staring intently up at the Museum windows. It was a tropically hot afternoon and they stood in deepest shadow. No one else was in Orchard Street—that odd little backwater—at the time, and they stood gazing upward intently and gave me not even a passing glance.

But I knew one for the Oriental visitor of the morning, and despite broad noonday and the hum of busy London about me, my blood seemed to turn to water. I stood rooted to the spot, held there by a most surprising horror.

For the gray-bearded figure of the other watcher was one I could never forget; its benignity was associated with the most horrible hours of my life, with deeds so dreadful that recollection to this day sometimes breaks my sleep, arousing me in the still watches, bathed in a cold sweat of fear.

It was Hassan of Aleppo!

If he saw me, if either of them saw me, I cannot say. What I should have done, what I might have done it is useless to speak of here—for I did nothing. Inert, thralled by the presence of that eerie, dreadful being, I watched them leave the shadow of the doorway and pace slowly on with their dignified Eastern gait.

Then, knowing how I had failed in my plain duty to my fellow-men—how, finding a serpent in my path, I had hesitated to crush it, had weakly succumbed to its uncanny fascination—I made my way round to the door of the Museum.

CHAPTER XIII
THE WHITE BEAM

That night the deviltry began. Mr. Mostyn found himself wholly unable to sleep. Many relics have curious histories, and the experienced archaeologist becomes callous to that uncanniness which seems to attach to some gruesome curios. But the slipper of the Prophet was different. No mere ghostly menace threatened its holders; an avenging scimitar followed those who came in contact with it; gruesome tragedies, mutilations, murders, had marked its progress throughout.

The night was still—as still as a London night can be; for there is always a vague murmuring in the metropolis as though the sleeping city breathed gently and sometimes stirred in its sleep.

Then, distinct amid these usual nocturnal noises, rose another, unaccountable sound, a muffled crash followed by a musical tinkling.

Mostyn sprang up in bed, drew on a dressing-gown, and took from the small safe at his bed-head the Museum keys and a loaded revolver. A somewhat dishevelled figure, pale and wild-eyed, he made his way through the private door and into the ghostly precincts of the Museum. He did not hesitate, but ascended the stairs and unlocked the door of the Assyrian gallery.

Along its ghostly aisles he passed, and before the door which gave admittance to the Burton Room paused, fumbling a moment for the key.

Inside the room something was moving!

Mostyn was keenly alarmed; he knew that he must enter at once or never. He inserted the key in the lock, swung open the heavy door, stepped through and closed it behind him. He was a man of tremendous moral courage, for now,—alone in the apartment which harboured the uncanny relic, alone in the discharge of his duty, he stood with his back to the door trembling slightly, but with the idea of retreat finding no place in his mind.

One side of the room lay in blackest darkness; through the furthermost window of the other a faint yellowed luminance (the moonlight through the blind) spread upon the polished parquet flooring. But that which held the curator spell-bound—that which momentarily quickened into life the latent superstition, common to all mankind, was a beam of cold light which poured its effulgence fully upon the case containing the Prophet's slipper! Where the other exhibits lay either in utter darkness or semi-darkness this one it seemed was supernaturally picked out by this lunar searchlight!

It was ghostly-unnerving; but, the first dread of it passed, Mostyn recalled how during the day a hole inexplicably had been cut in that blind; he recalled that it had not been mended, but that the damaged blind had merely been rolled up again.

And as a dawning perception of the truth came to him, as falteringly he advanced a step toward the mystic beam, he saw that one side of the case had been shattered—he saw the broken glass upon the floor; and in the dense shadow behind and under the beam of light, vaguely he saw a dull red object.

It moved—it seemed to live! It moved away from the case and in the direction of the eastern windows.

"My God!" whispered Mostyn; "it's the Prophet's slipper!"

And wildly, blindly, he fired down the room. Later he knew that he had fired in panic, for nothing human was or could be in the place; yet his shot was not without effect. In the instant of its flash, something struck sharply against the dimly seen blind of one of the east windows; he heard the crash of broken glass.

He leapt to the switch and flooded the room with light. A fear of what it might hold possessed him, and he turned instantly.

Hard by the fragments of broken glass upon the floor and midway between the case and the first easterly window lay the slipper. A bell was ringing somewhere. His shot probably had aroused the attention of the policeman. Someone was clamouring upon the door of the Museum, too. Mostyn raced forward and raised the blind—that toward which the slipper had seemed to move.

The lower pane of the window was smashed. Blood was trickling down upon the floor from the jagged edges of the glass.

"Hullo there! Open the door! Open the door!"

Bells were going all over the place now; sounds of running footsteps came from below; but Mostyn stood staring at the broken window and at the solid iron bars which protected it without, which were intact, substantial—which showed him that nothing human could possibly have entered.

Yet the case was shattered, the holy slipper lay close beside him upon the floor, and from the broken window-pane blood was falling—drip-drip-drip…

That was the story as I heard it half an hour later. For Inspector Bristol, apprised of the happening, was promptly on the scene; and knowing how keen was my interest in the matter, he rang me up immediately. I arrived soon after Bristol and found a perplexed group surrounding the uncanny slipper of the Prophet. No one had dared to touch it; the dread vengeance of Hassan of Aleppo would visit any unbeliever who ventured to lay hand upon the holy, bloody thing. Well we knew it, and as though it had been a venomous scorpion we, a company of up-to-date, prosaic men of affairs, stood around that dilapidated markoob, and kept a respectful distance.

Mostyn, an odd figure in pyjamas and dressing-gown, turned his pale, intellectual face to me as I entered.

"It will have to be put back … secretly," he said.

His voice was very unsteady. Bristol nodded grimly and glanced at the two constables, who, with a plain-clothes man unknown to me, made up that midnight company.

"I'll do it, sir," said one of the constables suddenly.

"One moment"—Mostyn raised his hand!

In the ensuing silence I could hear the heavy breathing of those around me. We were all looking at the slipper, I think.

"Do you understand, fully," the curator continued, "the risk you run?"

"I think so, sir," answered the constable; "but I'm prepared to chance it."

"The hands," resumed Mostyn slowly, "of those who hitherto have ventured to touch it have been"—he hesitated—"cut off."

"Your career in the Force would be finished if it happened to you, my lad," said Bristol shortly.

"I suppose they'd look after me," said the man, with grim humour.

"They would if you met with—an accident, in the discharge of your duty," replied the inspector; "but I haven't ordered you to do it, and I'm not going to."

"All right, sir," said the man, with a sort of studied truculence, "I'll take my chance."

I tried to stop him; Mostyn, too, stepped forward, and Bristol swore frankly. But it was all of no avail.

A sort of chill seemed to claim my very soul when I saw the constable stoop, unconcernedly pick up the slipper, and replace it in the broken case.

It was out of a silence cathedral-like, awesome, that he spoke.

"All you want is a new pane of glass, sir," he said—"and the thing's done."

I anticipate in mentioning it here; but since Constable Hughes has no further place in these records I may perhaps be excused for dismissing him at this point.

He was picked up outside the section house on the following evening with his right hand severed just above the wrist.

CHAPTER XIV
A SCREAM IN THE NIGHT

The day that followed was one of the hottest which we experienced during the heat wave. It was a day crowded with happenings. The Burton Room was closed to the public, whilst a glazier worked upon the broken east window and a new blind was fitted to the west. Behind the workmen, guarded by a watchful commissionaire, yawned the shattered case containing the slipper.

I wondered if the visitors to the other rooms of the Museum realized, as I realized, that despite the blazing sunlight of tropical London, the shadow of Hassan of Aleppo lay starkly on that haunted building?

At about eleven o'clock, as I hurried along the Strand, I almost collided with the girl of the violet eyes! She turned and ran like the wind down Arundel Street, whilst I stood at the corner staring after her in blank amazement, as did other passers-by; for a man cannot with dignity race headlong after a pretty woman down a public thoroughfare!

My mystification grew hourly deeper; and Bristol wallowed in perplexities.

"It's the most horrible and confusing case," he said to me when I joined him at the Museum, "that the Yard has ever had to handle. It bristles with outrages and murders. God knows where it will all end. I've had London scoured for a clue to the whereabouts of Hassan and Company and drawn absolutely blank! Then there's Earl Dexter. Where does he come in? For once in a way he's living in hiding. I can't find his headquarters. I've been thinking—"

He drew me aside into the small gallery which runs parallel with the Assyrian Room.

"Dexter has booked two passages in the Oceanic. Who is his companion?"

I wondered, I had wondered more than once, if his companion were my beautiful violet-eyed acquaintance. A scruple—perhaps an absurd scruple—

hitherto had kept me silent respecting her, but now I determined to take Bristol fully into my confidence. A conviction was growing upon me that she and Earl Dexter together represented that third party whose existence we had long suspected. Whether they operated separately or on behalf of the Moslems (of which arrangement I could not conceive) remained to be seen. I was about to voice my doubts and suspicions when Bristol went on hurriedly—

"I have thoroughly examined the Burton Room, and considering that the windows are thirty feet from the ground, that there is no sign of a ladder having stood upon the lawn, and that the iron bars are quite intact, it doesn't look humanly possible for any one to have been in the room last night prior to Mostyn's arrival!"

"One of the dwarfs—"

"Not even one of the dwarfs," said Bristol, "could have passed between those iron bars!"

"But there was blood on the window!"

"I know there was, and human blood. It's been examined!"

He stared at me fixedly. The thing was unspeakably uncanny.

"To-night," he went on, "I am remaining in here"—nodding toward the Assyrian Room—"and I have so arranged it that no mortal being can possibly know I am here. Mostyn is staying, and you can stay, too, if you care to. Owing to Professor Deeping's will you are badly involved in the beastly business, and I have no doubt you are keen to see it through."

"I am," I admitted, "and the end I look for and hope for is the recovery of the slipper by its murderous owners!"

"I am with you," said Bristol. "It's just a point of honour; but I should be glad to make them a present of it. We're ostentatiously placing a constable on duty in the hallway to-night—largely as a blind. It will appear that we're taking no other additional precautions."

He hurried off to make arrangements for my joining him in his watch, and thus again I lost my opportunity of confiding in him regarding the mysterious girl.

I half anticipated, though I cannot imagine why, that Earl Dexter would put in an appearance, during the day. He did not do so, however, for Bristol had put a constable on the door who was well acquainted with the appearance of The Stetson Man. The inspector, in the course of his investigations, had come upon what might have been a clue, but what was at best a confusing one. Close by the wall of the curator's house and lying on the gravel path he had found a part of a gold cuff link. It was of American manufacture.

Upon such slender evidence we could not justly assume that it pointed to the presence of Dexter on the night of the attempted robbery, but it served to complicate a matter already sufficiently involved.

In pursuance of Bristol's plan, I concealed myself that evening just before the closing of the Museum doors, in a recess behind a heavy piece of Babylonian sculpture. Bristol was similarly concealed in another part of the room, and Mostyn joined us later.

The Museum was closed; and so far as evidence went the authorities had relied again upon the bolts and bars hitherto considered impregnable, and upon the constable in the hall. The broken window was mended, the cut blind replaced, and within, in its shattered case, reposed the slipper of the Prophet.

All the blinds being lowered, the Assyrian Room was a place of gloom, yellowed on the western side by the moonlight through the blind. The door communicating with the Burton Room was closed but not fastened.

"They operated last night," Bristol whispered to me, "at the exact time when the moonlight shone through the hole in the westerly blind on to the case. If they come to-night, and I am quite expecting them, they will have to dispense with that assistance; but they know by experience where to reach the case."

"Despite our precautions," I said, "they will almost certainly know that a watch is being kept."

"They may or they may not," replied Bristol. "Either way I'm disposed to think there will be another attempt. Their mysterious method is so rapid that they can afford to take chances."

This was not my first night vigil since I had become in a sense the custodian of the relic, but it was quite the most dreary. Amid the tomb-like objects about us we seemed two puny mortals toying with stupendous things. We could not smoke and must converse only in whispers; and so the night wore on until I began to think that our watch would be dully uneventful.

"Our big chance," whispered Mostyn, "is in the fact that any day may change the conditions. They can't afford to wait."

He ceased abruptly, grasping my arm. From somewhere, somewhere outside the building, we all three had heard a soft whistle. A moment of tense listening followed.

"If only we could have had the place surrounded," whispered Bristol—"but it was impossible, of course."

A faint grating noise echoed through the lofty Burton Room. Bristol slipped past me in the semi-gloom, and gently opened the communicating door a few inches.

A-tiptoe, I joined him, and craning across his shoulder saw a strange and wonderful thing.

The newly glazed east window again was shattered with a booming crash! The yellow blind was thrust aside. A long something reached out toward the broken case. There was a sort of fumbling sound, and paralyzed with the wonder of it—for the window, remember, was thirty feet from the ground—I stood frozen to my post.

Not so Bristol. As the weird tentacle (or more exactly it reminded me of a gigantic crab's claw) touched the case, the Inspector leapt forward. A white beam from his electric torch cut through to the broken cabinet.

The thing was withdrawn ... and with it went the slipper of the Prophet.

"Raise the blinds!" cried Bristol. "Mr. Cavanagh! Mr. Mostyn! We must not let them give us the slip!"

I got up the blind of the nearer window as Bristol raised the other. Not a living thing was in sight from either!

Mostyn was beside me, his hand resting on my shoulder. I noted how he trembled. Bristol turned and looked back at us. The light from his pocket torch flashed upon the curator's face; and I have never seen such an expression of horrified amazement as that which it wore. Faintly, I could hear the constable racing up the steps from the hall.

Ideas of the supernatural came to us all, I know; when, with a scuffling sound not unlike that of a rat in a ceiling, something moved above us!

"Damn my thick head!" roared Bristol, furiously. "He's on the roof! It's flat as a floor and there's enough ivy alongside the water-spout on your house adjoining, Mr. Mostyn, to afford foothold to an invading army!"

He plunged off toward the open door, and I heard him racing down the Assyrian Room.

"He had a short rope ladder fixed from the gutter!" he cried back at us. "Graham! Graham!" (the constable on duty in the hall)—"Get the front door open! Get..." His voice died away as he leapt down the stairs.

From the direction of Orpington Square came a horrid, choking scream. It rose hideously; it fell, rose again—and died.

The thief escaped. We saw the traces upon the ivy where he had hastened down. Bristol ascended by the same route, and found where the ladder-hooks had twice been attached to the gutterway. Constable Graham, who was first actually to leave the building, declared that he heard the whirr of a re-started motor lower down Great Orchard Street.

Bristol's theory, later to be dreadfully substantiated, was that the thief had broken the glass and reached into the case with an arrangement similar to that employed for pruning trees, having a clutch at the end, worked with a cord.

"Hassan has been too clever for us!" said the inspector. "But—what in God's name did that awful screaming mean?"

I had a theory, but I did not advance it then.

It was not until nearly dawn that my theory, and Bristol's, regarding the clutch arrangement, both were confirmed. For close under the railings which abut on Orpington Square, in a pool of blood we found just such an instrument as Bristol had described.

And still clutching it was a pallid and ghastly shrunken hand that had been severed from above the wrist!

"Merciful God!" whispered the inspector—"look at the opal ring on the finger! Look at the bandage where he cut himself on the broken window-glass that first night, when Mr. Mostyn disturbed him. It wasn't the Hashishin who stole the thing.... It's Earl Dexter's hand!"

No one spoke for a moment. Then—

"Which of them has—" began Mostyn huskily.

"The slipper of the Prophet?" interrupted Bristol. "I wonder if we shall ever know?"

CHAPTER XV
A SHRIVELLED HAND

Around a large square table in a room at New Scotland Yard stood a group of men, all of whom looked more or less continuously at something that lay upon the polished deal. One of the party, none other than the Commissioner himself, had just finished speaking, and in silence now we stood about the gruesome object which had furnished him with the text of his very terse address.

I knew myself privileged in being admitted to such a conference at the C.I.D. headquarters and owed my admission partly to Inspector Bristol, and partly to the fact that under the will of the late Professor Deeping I was concerned in the uncanny business we were met to discuss.

Novelty has a charm for every one; and to find oneself immersed in a maelstrom of Eastern devilry, with a group of scientific murderers in pursuit of a holy Moslem relic, and unexpectedly to be made a trustee of that dangerous curiosity, makes a certain appeal to the adventurous. But to read of such things and to participate in them are widely different matters. The slipper of the Prophet and the dreadful crimes connected with it, the mutilations, murders, the uncanny mysteries which made up its history, were filling my world with horror.

Now, in silence we stood around that table at New Scotland Yard and watched, as though we expected it to move, the ghastly "clue" which lay there. It was a shrivelled human hand, and about the thumb and forefinger there still dryly hung a fragment of lint which had bandaged a jagged wound. On one of the shrunken fingers was a ring set with a large opal.

Inspector Bristol broke the oppressive silence.

"You see, sir," he said, addressing the Commissioner, "this marks a new complication in the case. Up to this week although, unfortunately, we had made next to no progress, the thing was straightforward enough. A band of Eastern murderers, working along lines quite novel to Europe, were concealed somewhere in London. We knew that much. They murdered Professor Deeping, but failed to recover the slipper. They mutilated everyone who touched it mysteriously. The best men in the department, working night and day, failed to effect a single arrest. In spite of the mysterious activity of Hassan of Aleppo the slipper was safely lodged in the British Antiquarian Museum."

The Commissioner nodded thoughtfully.

"There is no doubt," continued Bristol, "that the Hashishin were watching the Museum. Mr. Cavanagh, here"—he nodded in my direction—"saw Hassan himself lurking in the neighbourhood. We took every precaution, observed the greatest secrecy; but in spite of it all a constable who touched the accursed thing lost his right hand. Then the slipper was taken."

He stopped, and all eyes again were turned to the table.

"The Yard," resumed Bristol slowly, "had information that Earl Dexter, the cleverest crook in America, was in England. He was seen in the Museum, and the night following the slipper was stolen. Then outside the place I found—that!"

He pointed to the severed hand. No one spoke for a moment. Then—

"The new problem," said the Commissioner, "is this: who took the slipper, Dexter or Hassan of Aleppo?"

"That's it, sir," agreed Bristol. "Dexter had two passages booked in the Oceanic: but he didn't sail with her, and—that's his hand!"

"You say he has not been traced?" asked the Commissioner.

"No doctor known to the Medical Association," replied Bristol, "is attending him! He's not in any of the hospitals. He has completely vanished. The conclusion is obvious!"

"The evident deduction," I said, "is that Dexter stole the slipper from the Museum—God knows with what purpose—and that Hassan of Aleppo recovered it from him."

"You think we shall next hear of Earl Dexter from the river police?" suggested Bristol.

"Personally," replied the Commissioner, "I agree with Mr. Cavanagh. I think Dexter is dead, and it is very probable that Hassan and Company are already homeward bound with the slipper of the Prophet."

With all my heart I hoped that he might be right, but an intuition was with me crying that he was wrong, that many bloody deeds would be, ere the sacred slipper should return to the East.

CHAPTER XVI
THE DWARF

The manner in which we next heard of the whereabouts of the Prophet's slipper was utterly unforeseen, wildly dramatic. That the Hashishin were aware that I, though its legal trustee, no longer had charge of the relic nor knowledge of its resting-place, was sufficiently evident from the immunity which I enjoyed at this time from that ceaseless haunting by members of the uncanny organization ruled by Hassan. I had begun to feel more secure in my chambers, and no longer worked with a loaded revolver upon the table beside me. But the slightest unusual noise in the night still sufficed to arouse me and set me listening intently, to chill me with dread of what it might portend. In short, my nerves were by no means recovered from the ceaseless strain of the events connected with and arising out of the death of my poor friend, Professor Deeping.

One evening as I sat at work in my chambers, with the throb of busy Fleet Street and its thousand familiar sounds floating in to me through the open windows, my phone bell rang.

Even as I turned to take up the receiver a foreboding possessed me that my trusteeship was no longer to be a sinecure. It was Bristol who had rung me up, and upon very strange business.

"A development at last!" he said; "but at present I don't know what to make of it. Can you come down now?"

"Where are you speaking from?"

"From the Waterloo Road—a delightful neighbourhood. I shall be glad if you can meet me at the entrance to Wyatt's Buildings in half an hour."

"What is it? Have you found Dexter?"

"No, unfortunately. But it's murder!"

I knew as I hung up the receiver that my brief period of peace was ended; that the lists of assassination were reopened. I hurried out through the court into Fleet Street, thinking of the key of the now empty case at the Museum which reposed at my bankers, thinking of the devils who pursued the slipper, thinking of the hundred and one things, strange and terrible, which went to make up the history of that gruesome relic.

Wyatt's Buildings, Waterloo Road, are a gloomy and forbidding block of dwellings which seem to frown sullenly upon the high road, from which they are divided by a dark and dirty courtyard. Passing an iron gateway, you enter, by way of an arch, into this sinister place of uncleanness. Male residents in their shirt sleeves lounge against the several entrances. Bedraggled women nurse dirty infants and sit in groups upon the stone steps, rendering them almost impassable. But to-night a thing had happened in Wyatt's Buildings which had awakened in the inhabitants, hardened to sordid crime, a sort of torpid interest.

Faces peered from most of the windows which commanded a view of the courtyard, looking like pallid blotches against the darkness; but a number of police confined the loungers within their several doorways, so that the yard itself was comparatively clear.

I had had some difficulty in forcing a way through the crowd which thronged the entrance, but finally I found myself standing beside Inspector Bristol and looking down upon that which had brought us both to Wyatt's Buildings.

There was no moon that night, and only the light of the lamp in the archway, with some faint glimmers from the stairways surrounding the court, reached the dirty paving. Bristol directed the light of a pocket-lamp upon the hunched-up figure which lay in the dust, and I saw it to be that of a dwarfish creature, yellow skinned and wearing only a dark loin cloth. He had a malformed and disproportionate head, a head that had been too large even for a big man. I knew after first glance that this was one of the horrible dwarfs employed by the Hashishin in their murderous business. It might even be the one who had killed Deeping; but this was impossible to determine by reason of the fact that the hideous, swollen head, together with the features, was completely crushed. I shall not describe the creature's appearance in further detail.

Having given me an opportunity to examine the dead dwarf, Bristol returned the electric lamp to his pocket and stood looking at me in the semi-gloom. A constable stood on duty quite near to us, and others guarded the archway and the doors to the dwellings. The murmur of subdued voices echoed hollowly in the wells of the staircases, and a constant excited murmur proceeded from the crowd at the entrance. No pressmen had yet been admitted, though numbers of them were at the gates.

"It happened less than an hour ago," said Bristol. "The place was much as you see it now, and from what I can gather there came the sound of a shot and several people saw the dwarf fall through the air and drop where he lies!"

The light was insufficient to show the expression upon the speaker's face, but his voice told of a great wonder.

"It is a bit like an Indian conjuring trick," I said, looking up to the sky above us; "who fired the shot?"

"So far," replied Bristol, "I have failed to find out; but there's a bullet in the thing's head. He was dead before he reached the pavement."

"Did no one see the flash of the pistol?"

"No one that I have got hold of yet. Of course this kind of evidence is very unreliable; these people regularly go out of their way to mislead the police."

"You think the body may have been carried here from somewhere else?"

"Oh, no; this is where it fell, right enough. You can see where his head struck the stones."

"He has not been moved at all?"

"No; I shall not move him until I've worked out where in heaven's name he can have fallen from! You and I have seen some mysterious things happen, Mr. Cavanagh, since the slipper of the Prophet came to England and brought these people"—he nodded toward the thing at our feet—"in its train; but this is the most inexplicable incident to date. I don't know what to make of it at all. Quite apart from the question of where the dwarf fell from, who shot at him and why?"

"Have you no theory?" I asked. "The incident to my mind points directly to one thing. We know that this uncanny creature belonged to the organization of Hassan of Aleppo. We know that Hassan implacably pursues one object—the slipper. In pursuit of the slipper, then, the dwarf came here. Bristol!"—I laid my hand upon his arm, glancing about me with a very real apprehension—"the slipper must be somewhere near!"

Bristol turned to the constable standing hard by.

"Remain here," he ordered. Then to me: "I should like you to come up on to the roof. From there we can survey the ground and perhaps arrive at some explanation of how the dwarf came to fall upon that spot."

Passing the constable on duty at one of the doorways and making our way through the group of loiterers there, we ascended amid conflicting odours to the topmost floor. A ladder was fixed against the wall communicating with a trap in the ceiling. Several individuals in their shirt sleeves and all smoking clay pipes had followed us up. Bristol turned upon them.

"Get downstairs," he said—"all the lot of you, and stop there!"

With muttered imprecations our audience dispersed, slowly returning by the way they had come. Bristol mounted the ladder and opened the trap. Through the square opening showed a velvet patch spangled with starry points. As he passed up on to the roof and I followed him, the comparative cleanness of the air was most refreshing after the varied fumes of the staircase.

Side by side we leaned upon the parapet looking down into the dirty courtyard which was the theatre of this weird mystery; looking down upon the stage, sordidly Western, where a mystic Eastern tragedy had been enacted.

I could see the constable standing beside the crushed thing upon the stones.

"Now," said Bristol, with a sort of awe in his voice, "where did he fall from?"

And at his words, looking down at the spot where the dwarf lay, and noting that he could not possibly have fallen there from any of the buildings surrounding the courtyard, an eerie sensation crept over me; for I was convinced that the happening was susceptible of no natural explanation.

I had heard—who has not heard?—of the Indian rope trick, where a fakir throws a rope into the air which remains magically suspended whilst a boy climbs upward and upward until he disappears into space. I had never credited accounts of the performance; but now I began seriously to wonder if the arts of Hassan of Aleppo were not as great or greater than the arts of fakir. But the crowning mystery to my mind was that of the Hashishin's death. It would seem that as he had hung suspended in space he had been shot!

"You say that someone heard the sound of the shot?" I asked suddenly.

"Several people," replied Bristol; "but no one knows, or no one will say, from what direction it came. I shall go on with the inquiry, of course, and cross-examine every soul in Wyatt's Buildings. Meanwhile, I'm open to confess that I am beaten."

In the velvet sky countless points blazed tropically. The hum of the traffic in Waterloo Road reached us only in a muffled way. Sordidness lay beneath us, but up there under the heavens we seemed removed from it as any Babylonian astronomer communing with the stars.

When, some ten minutes later, I passed out into the noise of Waterloo Road, I left behind me an unsolved mystery and took with me a great dread; for I knew that the quest of the sacred slipper was not ended, I knew that another tragedy was added to its history—and I feared to surmise what the future might hold for all of us.

CHAPTER XVII
THE WOMAN WITH THE BASKET

Deep in thought respecting the inexplicable nature of this latest mystery, I turned in the direction of the bridge, and leaving behind me an ever-swelling throng at the gate of Wyatt's Buildings, proceeded westward.

The death of the dwarf had lifted the case into the realms of the marvellous, and I noted nothing of the bustle about me, for mentally I was still surveying that hunched-up body which had fallen out of empty space.

Then in upon my preoccupation burst a woman's scream!

I aroused myself from reverie, looking about to right and left. Evidently I had been walking slowly, for I was less than a hundred yards from Wyatt's Buildings, and hard by the entrance to an uninviting alley from which I thought the scream had proceeded.

And as I hesitated, for I had no desire to become involved in a drunken brawl, again came the shrill scream: "Help! help!"

I cannot say if I was the only passer-by who heard the cry; certainly I was the only one who responded to it. I ran down the narrow street, which was practically deserted, and heard windows thrown up as I passed for the cries for help continued.

Just beyond a patch of light cast by a street lamp a scene was being enacted strange enough at any time and in any place, but doubly singular at that hour of the night, or early morning, in a lane off the Waterloo Road.

An old woman, from whose hand a basket of provisions had fallen, was struggling in the grasp of a tall Oriental! He was evidently trying to stifle her screams and at the same time to pinion her arms behind her!

I perceived that there was more in this scene than met the eye. Oriental footpads are rarities in the purlieus of Waterloo Road. So much was evident;

and since I carried a short, sharp argument in my pocket, I hastened to advance it.

At the sight of the gleaming revolver barrel the man, who was dressed in dark clothes and wore a turban, turned and ran swiftly off. I had scarce a glimpse of his pallid brown face ere he was gone, nor did the thought of pursuit enter my mind. I turned to the old woman, who was dressed in shabby black and who was rearranging her thick veil in an oddly composed manner, considering the nature of the adventure that had befallen her.

She picked up her basket, and turned away. Needless to say I was rather shocked at her callous ingratitude, for she offered no word of thanks, did not even glance in my direction, but made off hurriedly toward Waterloo Road.

I had been on the point of inquiring if she had sustained any injury, but I checked the words and stood looking after her in blank wonderment. Then my ideas were diverted into a new channel. I perceived, as she passed under an adjacent lamp, that her basket contained provisions such as a woman of her appearance would scarcely be expected to purchase. I noted a bottle of wine, a chicken, and a large melon.

The nationality of the assailant from the first had marked the affair for no ordinary one, and now a hazy notion of what lay behind all this began to come to me.

Keeping well in the shadows on the opposite side of the way, I followed the woman with the basket. The lane was quite deserted; for, the disturbance over, those few residents who had raised their windows had promptly lowered them again. She came out into Waterloo Road, crossed over, and stood waiting by a stopping-place for electric cars. I saw her arranging a cloth over her basket in such a way as effectually to conceal the contents. A strong mental excitement possessed me. The detective fever claims us all at one time or another, I think, and I had good reason for pursuing any inquiry that promised to lead to the elucidation of the slipper mystery. A theory, covering all the facts of the assault incident, now presented itself, and I stood back in the shadow, watchful; in a degree, exultant.

A Greenwich-bound car was hailed by the woman with the basket. I could not be mistaken, I felt sure, in my belief that she cast furtive glances about her as she mounted the steps. But, having seen her actually aboard, my attention became elsewhere engaged.

All now depended upon securing a cab before the tram car had passed from view!

I counted it an act of Providence that a disengaged taxi appeared at that moment, evidently bound for Waterloo Station. I ran out into the road with cane upraised.

As the man drew up—

"Quick!" I cried. "You see that Greenwich car—nearly at the Ophthalmic Hospital? Follow it. Don't get too near. I will give you further instructions through the tube." I leapt in. We were off!

The rocking car ahead was rounding the bend now toward St. George's Circus. As it passed the clock and entered South London Road it stopped. I raised the tube.

"Pass it slowly!"

We skirted the clock tower, and bore around to the right. Then I drew well back in the corner of the cab.

The woman with the basket was descending! "Pull up a few yards beyond!" I directed. As the car re-started, and passed us, the taxi became stationary. I peered out of the little window at the back.

The woman was returning in the direction of Waterloo Road!

"Drive slowly back along Waterloo Road," was my next order. "Pretend you are looking for a fare; I will keep out of sight."

The man nodded. It was unlikely that any one would notice the fact that the cab was engaged.

I was borne back again upon my course. The woman kept to the right, and, once we were entered into the straight road which leads to the bridge, I again raised the speaking-tube.

"Pull up," I said. "On the right-hand side is an old woman carrying a basket, fifty yards ahead. Do you see her? Keep well behind, but don't lose sight of her."

The man drew up again and sat watching the figure with the basket until it was almost lost from sight. Then slowly we resumed our way. I would have continued the pursuit afoot now, but I feared that my quarry might again enter a vehicle. She did not do so, however, but coming abreast of the turning in which the mysterious assault had taken place, she crossed the road and disappeared from view.

I leapt out of the cab, thrust half a crown into the man's hand, and ran on to the corner. The night was now far advanced, and I knew that the chances of detection were thereby increased. But the woman seemed to have abandoned her fears, and I saw her just ahead of me walking resolutely past the lamp beyond which a short time earlier she had met with a dangerous adventure.

Since the opposite side of the street was comparatively in darkness, I slipped across, and in a state of high nervous tension pursued this strange work of espionage. I was convinced that I had forestalled Bristol and that I was hot upon the track of those who could explain the mystery of the dead dwarf.

The woman entered the gate of the block of dwellings even more forbidding in appearance than those which that night had staged a dreadful drama.

As the figure with the basket was lost from view I crept on, and in turn entered the evil-smelling hallway. I stepped cautiously, and standing beneath a gaslight protected by a wire frame, I congratulated myself upon having reached that point of vantage as silently as any Sioux stalker.

Footsteps were receding up the stone stairs. Craning my neck, I peered up the well of the staircase. I could not see the woman, but from the sound of her tread it was possible to count the landings which she passed. When she had reached the fourth, and I heard her step upon yet another flight, I knew that she must be bound for the topmost floor; and observing every precaution, almost holding my breath in a nervous endeavour to make not the slightest sound, rapidly I mounted the stairs.

I was come to the third landing in this secret fashion when quite distinctly I heard the grating of a key in a lock!

Since four doors opened upon each of the landings, at all costs, I thought, I must learn by which door she entered.

Throwing caution to the winds I raced up the remaining flights ... and there at the top the woman confronted me, with blazing eyes!—with eyes that thrilled every nerve; for they were violet eyes, the only truly violet eyes I have ever seen! They were the eyes of the woman who like a charming, mocking will-o'-the-wisp had danced through this tragic scene from the time that poor Professor Deeping had brought the Prophet's slipper to London up to this present hour!

There at the head of those stone steps in that common dwelling-house I knew her—and in the violet eyes it was written that she knew, and feared, me!

"What do you want? Why are you following me?"

She made no endeavour to disguise her voice. Almost, I think, she spoke the words involuntarily.

I stood beside her. Quickly as she had turned from the door at my ascent, I had noted that it was that numbered forty-eight which she had been about to open.

"You waste words," I said grimly. "Who lives there?"

I nodded in the direction of the doorway. The violet eyes watched me with an expression in their depths which I find myself wholly unable to describe. Fear predominated, but there was anger, too, and with it a sort of entreaty which almost made me regret that I had taken this task upon myself. From beneath the shabby black hat escaped an errant lock of wavy hair wholly inconsistent with the assumed appearance of the woman. The flickering gaslight on the landing sought out in that wonderful hair shades which seemed to glow with the soft light seen in the heart of a rose. The thick veil was raised now and all attempts at deception abandoned. At bay she faced me, this secret woman whom I knew to hold the key to some of the darkest places which we sought to explore.

"I live there," she said slowly. "What do you want with me?"

"I want to know," I replied, "for whom are those provisions in your basket?"

She watched me fixedly.

"And I want to know," I continued, "something that only you can tell me. We have met before, madam, but you have always eluded me. This time you shall not do so. There's much I have to ask of you, but particularly I want to know who killed the Hashishin who lies dead at no great distance from here!"

"How can I tell you that? Of what are you speaking?"

Her voice was low and musical; that of a cultured woman. She evidently recognized the futility of further subterfuge in this respect.

"You know quite well of what I am speaking! You know that you can tell me if any one can! The fact that you go disguised alone condemns you! Why should I remind you of our previous meetings—of the links which bind you to the history of the Prophet's slipper?" She shuddered and closed her eyes. "Your present attitude is a sufficient admission!"

She stood silent before me, with something pitiful in her pose—a wonderfully pretty woman, whose disarranged hair and dilapidated hat could not mar her beauty; whose clumsy, ill-fitting garments could not conceal her lithe grace.

Our altercation had not thus far served to arouse any of the inhabitants and on that stuffy landing, beneath the flickering gaslight, we stood alone, a group of two which epitomized strange things.

Then, with that quietly dramatic note which marks real life entrances and differentiates them from the loudly acclaimed episodes of the stage, a third actor took up his cue.

"Both hands, Mr. Cavanagh!" directed an American voice.

Nerves atwitch, I started around in its direction.

From behind the slightly opened door of No. 48 protruded a steel barrel, pointed accurately at my head!

I hesitated, glancing from the woman toward the open door.

"Do it quick!" continued the voice incisively. "You are up against a desperate man, Mr. Cavanagh. Raise your hands. Carneta, relieve Mr. Cavanagh of his gun!"

Instantly the girl, with deft fingers, had obtained possession of my revolver.

"Step inside," said the crisp, strident voice. Knowing myself helpless and quite convinced that I was indeed in the clutches of desperate people, I entered the doorway, the door being held open from within. She whom I had heard called Carneta followed. The door was reclosed; and I found myself in a perfectly bare and dim passageway. From behind me came the order—

"Go right ahead!"

Into a practically unfurnished room, lighted by one gas jet, I walked. Some coarse matting hung before the two windows and a fairly large grip stood on the floor against one wall. A gas-ring was in the hearth, together with a few cheap cooking utensils.

I turned and faced the door. First entered Carneta, carrying the basket; then came a man with a revolver in his left hand and his right arm strapped across his chest and swathed in bandages. One glance revealed the fact that his right hand had been severed—revealed the fact, though I knew it already, that my captor was Earl Dexter.

He looked even leaner than when I had last seen him. I had no doubt that his ghastly wound had occasioned a tremendous loss of blood. His gaunt face was positively emaciated, but the steely gray eyes had lost nothing of their brightness. There was a good deal about Mr. Earl Dexter, the cracksman, that any man must have admired.

"Shut the door, Carneta," he said quietly. His companion closed the door and Dexter sat down on the grip, regarding me with his oddly humorous smile.

"You're a visitor I did not expect, Mr. Cavanagh," he said. "I expected someone worse. You've interfered a bit with my plans but I don't know that I can't rearrange things satisfactorily. I don't think I'll stop for supper, though—" He glanced at the girl, who stood silent by the door.

"Just pack up the provisions," he directed, nodding toward the basket—"in the next room."

She departed without a word.

"That's a noticeable dust coat you're wearing, Mr. Cavanagh," said the American; "it gives me a great notion. I'm afraid I'll have to borrow it."

He glanced, smiling, at the revolver in his left hand and back again to me. There was nothing of the bully about him, nothing melodramatic; but I took off the coat without demur and threw it across to him.

"It will hide this stump," he said grimly; "and any of the Hashishin gentlemen who may be on the look-out—though I rather fancy the road is clear at the moment—will mistake me for you. See the idea? Carneta will be in a cab and I'll be in after her and away before they've got time to so much as whistle."

Very awkwardly he got into the coat.

"She's a clever girl, Carneta," he said. "She's doctored me all along since those devils cut my hand off."

As he finished speaking Carneta returned.

She had discarded her rags and wore a large travelling coat and a fashionable hat.

"Ready?" asked Dexter. "We'll make a rush for it. We meant to go to-night anyway. It's getting too hot here!" He turned to me.

"Sorry to say," he drawled, "I'll have to tie you up and gag you. Apologize; but it can't be helped."

Carneta nodded and went out of the room again, to return almost immediately with a line that looked as though it might have been employed for drying washing.

"Hands behind you," rapped Dexter, toying with the revolver—"and think yourself lucky you've got two!"

There was no mistaking the manner of man with whom I had to deal, and I obeyed; but my mind was busy with a hundred projects. Very neatly the girl bound my wrists, and in response to a slight nod from Dexter threw the end of the line up over a beam in the sloping ceiling, for the room was right under the roof, and drew it up in such a way that, my wrists being raised behind me, I became utterly helpless. It was an ingenious device indicating considerable experience.

"Just tie his handkerchief around his mouth," directed Dexter: "that will keep him quiet long enough for our purpose. I hope you will be released soon, Mr. Cavanagh," he added. "Greatly regret the necessity."

Carneta bound the handkerchief over my mouth.

Dexter extinguished the gas.

"Mr. Cavanagh," he said, "I've gone through hell and I've lost the most useful four fingers and a thumb in the United States to get hold of the Prophet's slipper. Any one can have it that's open to pay for it—but I've got to retire on the deal, so I'll drive a hard bargain! Good-night!"

There was a sound of retreating footsteps, and I heard the entrance door close quietly.

CHAPTER XVIII
WHAT CAME THROUGH THE WINDOW

I had not been in my unnatural position for many minutes before I began to suffer agonies, agonies not only physical but mental; for standing there like some prisoner of the Inquisition, it came to me how this dismantled apartment must be the focus of the dreadful forces of Hassan of Aleppo!

That Earl Dexter had the slipper of the Prophet I no longer doubted, and that he had sustained, in this dwelling beneath the roof, an uncanny siege during the days which had passed since the theft from the Antiquarian Museum, was equally certain. Helpless, gagged, I pictured those hideous creatures, evil products of the secret East, who might, nay, who must surround that place! I thought of the horrible little yellow man who lay dead in Wyatt's Buildings; and it became evident to me that the house in which I was now imprisoned must overlook the back of those unsavoury tenements. The windows, sack-covered now, no doubt commanded a view of the roofs of the buildings. One of the mysteries that had puzzled us was solved. It was Earl Dexter who had shot the yellow dwarf as he was bound for this very room! But how humanly the Hashishin had proposed to gain his goal, how he had travelled through empty space—for from empty space the shot had brought him down—I could not imagine.

I knew something of the almost supernatural attributes of these people. From Professor Deeping's book I knew of the incredible feats which they could perform when under the influence of the drug hashish. From personal experience also I knew that they had powers wholly abnormal.

The pain in my arms and back momentarily increased. An awesome silence ruled. I tortured myself with pictures of murderous yellow men possessed of the power claimed by the Mahatmas, of levitation. Mentally I could see a distorted half-animal creature carrying a great gleaming knife and floating supernaturally toward me through the night!

A soft pattering sound became perceptible on the sloping roof above!

I think I have never known such intense and numbing fear as that which now descended upon me. Perhaps I may be forgiven it. A more dreadful situation it would be hard to devise. Knowing that I was on the fifth story of a house, bound, helpless, I knew, too, that a second mystic guardian of the slipper was come to accomplish the task in which the first had failed!

I began to pray fervently.

Neither of the windows were closed; and now through the intense darkness I heard one of them being raised up—up—up...

The sacking was pulled aside inch by inch.

Silhouetted against the faintly luminous background I saw a hunched, unnatural figure. The real was more dreadful even than the imaginary—for some stray beam of light touched into cold radiance a huge curved knife which the visitant held between his teeth!

My fear became a madness, and I twisted my body violently in a wild endeavour to free myself. A dreadful pain shot through my left shoulder, and the whole nightmare scene—the thing with the knife at the window—the low-ceiled room-began to fade away from me. I seemed to be falling into deep water.

A splintering crash and the sound of shouting formed my last recollections ere unconsciousness came.

I found myself lying in an armchair with Bristol forcing brandy between my lips. My left arm hung limply at my side and the pain in my dislocated shoulder was excruciating.

"Thank God you are all right, Mr. Cavanagh!" said the inspector. "I got the surprise of my life when we smashed the door in and found you tied up here!"

"You came none too soon," I said feebly. "God knows how Providence directed you here."

"Providence it was," replied Bristol. "From the roof of Wyatt's Buildings—you know the spot?—I saw the second yellow devil coming. By God! They meant to have it to-night! They don't value their lives a brass farthing against that damned slipper!"

"But how—"

"Along the telegraph-wires, Mr. Cavanagh! They cross Wyatt's Buildings and cross this house. It was a moonless night or we should have seen it at once! I watched him, saw him drop to this roof—and brought the men around to the front."

"Did he, that awful thing, escape?"

"He dropped full forty feet into a tree—from the tree to the ground, and went off like a cat!"

"Earl Dexter has escaped us," I said, "and he has the slipper!"

"God help him!" replied Bristol. "For by now he has that hell-pack at his heels! What a case! Heavens above, it will drive me mad!"

CHAPTER XIX
A RAPPING AT MIDNIGHT

Inspector Bristol finished his whisky at a gulp and stood up, a tall, massive figure, stretching himself and yawning.

"The detective of fiction would be hard at work on this case, now," he said, smiling, "but I don't even pretend to be. I am at a standstill and I don't care who knows it."

"You have absolutely no clue to the whereabouts of Earl Dexter?"

"Not the slightest, Mr. Cavanagh. You hear a lot about the machinery of the law, but as a matter of fact, looking for a clever man hidden in London is a good deal like looking for a needle in a haystack. Then, he may have been bluffing when he told you he had the Prophet's slipper. He's already had his hand cut off through interfering with the beastly thing, and I really can't believe he would take further chances by keeping it in his possession. Nevertheless, I should like to find him."

He leaned back against the mantelpiece, scratching his head perplexedly. In this perplexity he had my sympathy. No such pursuit, I venture to say, had ever before been required of Scotland Yard as this of the slipper of the Prophet. An organization founded in 1090, which has made a science of assassination, which through the centuries has perfected the malign arts, which, lingering on in a dark spot in Syria, has suddenly migrated and established itself in London, is a proposition almost unthinkable.

It was hard to believe that even the daring American cracksman should have ventured to touch that blood-stained relic of the Prophet, that he should have snatched it away from beneath the very eyes of the fanatics who fiercely guarded it. What he hoped to gain by his possession of the slipper was not evident, but the fact remained that if he could be believed, he had it, and provided Scotland Yard's information was accurate, he still lurked in hiding somewhere in London.

Meanwhile, no clue offered to his hiding-place, and despite the ceaseless vigilance of the men acting under Bristol's orders, no trace could be found of Hassan of Aleppo nor of his fiendish associates.

"My theory is," said Bristol, lighting a cigarette, "that even Dexter's cleverness has failed to save him. He's probably a dead man by now, which accounts for our failing to find him; and Hassan of Aleppo has recovered the slipper and returned to the East, taking his gruesome company with him—God knows how! But that accounts for our failing to find him."

I stood up rather wearily. Although poor Deeping had appointed me legal guardian of the relic, and although I could render but a poor account of my stewardship, let me confess that I was anxious to take that comforting theory to my bosom. I would have given much to have known beyond any possibility of doubt that the accursed slipper and its blood-lustful guardian were far away from England. Had I known so much, life would again have had something to offer me besides ceaseless fear, endless watchings. I could have slept again, perhaps; without awaking, clammy, peering into every shadow, listening, nerves atwitch to each slightest sound disturbing the night; without groping beneath the pillow for my revolver.

"Then you think," I said, "that the English phase of the slipper's history is closed? You think that Dexter, minus his right hand, has eluded British law—that Hassan and Company have evaded retribution?"

"I do!" said Bristol grimly, "and although that means the biggest failure in my professional career, I am glad—damned glad!"

Shortly afterward he took his departure; and I leaned from the window, watching him pass along the court below and out under the arch into Fleet Street. He was a man whose opinions I valued, and in all sincerity I prayed now that he might be right; that the surcease of horror which we had recently experienced after the ghastly tragedies which had clustered thick about the haunted slipper, might mean what he surmised it to mean.

The heat to-night was very oppressive. A sort of steaming mist seemed to rise from the court, and no cooling breeze entered my opened windows. The clamour of the traffic in Fleet Street came to me but remotely. Big Ben began to strike midnight. So far as I could see, residents on the other stairs were all abed and a velvet shadow carpet lay unbroken across three parts of the court. The sky was tropically perfect, cloudless, and jewelled lavishly. Indeed, we were in the midst of an Indian summer; it seemed that the uncanny visitants had brought, together with an atmosphere of black Eastern deviltry, something, too, of the Eastern climate.

The last stroke of the Cathedral bell died away. Other more distant bells still were sounding dimly, but save for the ceaseless hum of the traffic, no unusual sound now disturbed the archaic peace of the court.

I returned to my table, for during the time that had passed I had badly neglected my work and now must often labour far into the night. I was just reseated when there came a very soft rapping at the outer door!

No doubt my mood was in part responsible, but I found myself thinking of Poe's weird poem, "The Raven"; and like the character therein I found myself hesitating.

I stole quietly into the passage. It was in darkness. How odd it is that in moments of doubt instinctively one shuns the dark and seeks the light. I pressed the switch lighting the hall lamp, and stood looking at the closed door.

Why should this late visitor have rapped in so uncanny a fashion in preference to ringing the bell?

I stepped back to my table and slipped a revolver into my pocket.

The muffled rapping was repeated. As I stood in the study doorway I saw the flap of the letter-box slowly raised!

Instantly I extinguished both lights. You may brand me as childishly timid, but incidents were fresh in my memory which justified all my fears.

A faintly luminous slit in the door showed me that the flap was now fully raised. It was the dim light on the stairway shining through. Then quite silently the flap was lowered. Came the soft rapping again.

"Who's there?" I cried.

No one answered.

Wondering if I were unduly alarming myself, yet, I confess, strung up tensely in anticipation that this was some device of the phantom enemy, I stood in doubt.

The silence remained unbroken for thirty seconds or more. Then yet again it was disturbed by that ghostly, muffled rapping.

I advanced a step nearer to the door.

"Who's there?" I cried loudly. "What do you want?"

The flap of the letter box began to move, and I formed a sudden determination. Making no sound in my heelless Turkish slippers I crept close up to the door and dropped upon my knees.

Thereupon the flap became fully lifted, but from where I crouched beneath it I was unable to see who or what was looking in; yet I hesitated no longer. I suddenly raised myself and thrust the revolver barrel through the opening!

"Who are you?" I cried. "Answer or I fire!"—and along the barrel I peered out on to the landing.

Still no one answered. But something impalpable—a powder—a vapour—to this hour I do not know what—enveloped me with its nauseating fumes; was puffed fully into my face! My eyes, my mouth, my nostrils became choked up, it seemed, with a deadly stifling perfume.

Wildly, feeling that everything about me was slipping away, that I was sinking into a void, for ought I knew that of dissolution, I pulled the trigger once, twice, thrice…

"My God!"—the words choked in my throat and I reeled back into the passage—"it's not loaded!"

I threw up my arms to save myself, lurched, and fell forward into what seemed a bottomless pit.

CHAPTER XX
THE GOLDEN PAVILION

When I opened my eyes it was to a conviction that I dreamed. I lay upon a cushioned divan in a small apartment which I find myself at a loss adequately to describe.

It was a yellow room, then, its four walls being hung with yellow silk, its floor being entirely covered by a yellow Persian carpet. One lamp, burning in a frame of some lemon coloured wood and having its openings filled with green glass, flooded the place with a ghastly illumination. The lamp hung by gold chains from the ceiling, which was yellow. Several low tables of the same lemon-hued wood as the lamp-frame stood around; they were inlaid in fanciful designs with gleaming green stones. Turn my eyes where I would, clutch my aching head as I might, this dream chamber would not disperse, but remained palpable before me—yellow and green and gold.

There was a niche behind the divan upon which I lay framed about with yellow wood. In it stood a golden bowl and a tall pot of yellow porcelain; I lay amid yellow cushions having golden tassels. Some of them were figured with vivid green devices.

To contemplate my surroundings assuredly must be to court madness. No door was visible, no window; nothing but silk and luxury, yellow and green and gold.

To crown all, the air was heavy with a perfume wholly unmistakable by one acquainted with Egypt's ruling vice. It was the reek of smouldering hashish—a stench that seemed to take me by the throat, a vapour damnable and unclean. I saw that a little censer, golden in colour and inset with emeralds, stood upon the furthermost corner of the yellow carpet. From it rose a faint streak of vapour; and I followed the course of the sickly scented smoke upward through the still air until in oily spirals it lost itself near to the yellow ceiling. As a sick man will study the veriest trifle I studied that wisp of smoke, pencilled grayly against the silken draperies, the carven tables, against the almost terrifying persistency of the yellow and green and gold.

I strove to rise, but was overcome by vertigo and sank back again upon the yellow cushions. I closed my eyes, which throbbed and burned, and rested my head upon my hands. I ceased to conjecture if I dreamed or was awake. I knew that I felt weak and ill, that my head throbbed agonizingly, that my eyes smarted so as to render it almost impossible to keep them open, that a ceaseless humming was in my ears.

For some time I lay endeavouring to regain command of myself, to prepare to face again that scene which had something horrifying in its yellowness, touched with the green and gold.

And when finally I reopened my eyes, I sat up with a suppressed cry. For a tall figure in a yellow robe from beneath which peeped yellow slippers, a figure crowned with a green turban, stood in the centre of the apartment!

It was that of a majestic old man, white bearded, with aquiline nose, and the fierce eagle eyes of a fanatic set upon me sternly, reprovingly.

With folded arms he stood watching me, and I drew a sharp breath and rose slowly to my feet.

There amid the yellow and green and gold, amid the abominable reek of burning hashish I stood and faced Hassan of Aleppo!

No words came to me; I was confounded.

Hassan spoke in that gentle voice which I had heard only once before.

"Mr. Cavanagh," he said, "I have brought you here that I might warn you. Your police are seeking me night and day, and I am fully alive to my danger whilst I stay in your midst. But for close upon a thousand years the Sheikh-al-jebal, Lord of the Hashishin, has guarded the traditions and the relics of the Prophet, Salla-'llahu 'ale yhi wasellem! I, Hassan of Aleppo, am Sheikh of the Order to-day, and my sacred duty has brought me here."

The piercing gaze never left my face. I was not yet by any means my own man and still I made no reply.

"You have been wise," continued Hassan, "in that you have never touched the sacred slipper. Had you lain hands upon it, no secrecy could have availed you. The eye of the Hashishin sees all. There is a shaft of light which the true Believer perceives at night as he travels toward El-Medineh. It is the light which uprises, a spiritual fire, from the tomb of the Prophet (Salla-'llahu 'aleyhi wasellem!). The relics also are radiant, though in a lesser degree."

He took a step toward me, spreading out his lean brown hands, palms downward.

"A shaft of light," he said impressively, "shines upward now from London. It is the light of the holy slipper." He gazed intently at the yellow drapery at the left of the divan, but as though he were looking not at the wall but through it. His features worked convulsively; he was a man inspired. "I see it now!" he almost whispered—"that white light by which the guardians of the relic may always know its resting place!"

I managed to force words to my lips.

"If you know where the slipper is," I said, more for the sake of talking than for anything else, "why do you not recover it?"

Hassan turned his eyes upon me again.

"Because the infidel dog," he cried loudly, "who has soiled it with his unclean touch, defies us—mocks us! He has suffered the loss of the offending hand, but the evil ginn protect him; he is inspired by efreets! But God is great and Mohammed is His only Prophet! We shall triumph; but it is written, oh, daring infidel, that you again shall become the guardian of the slipper!"

He spoke like some prophet of old and I stared at him fascinated. I was loth to believe his words.

"When again," he continued, "the slipper shall be in the receptacle of which you hold the key, that key must be given to me!"

I thought I saw the drift of his words now; I thought I perceived with what object I had been trapped and borne to this mysterious abode for whose whereabouts the police vainly were seeking. By the exercise of the gift of divination it would seem that Hassan of Aleppo had forecast the future history of the accursed slipper or believed that he had done so. According to his own words I was doomed once more to become trustee of the relic. The key of the case at the Antiquarian Museum, to which he had prophesied the slipper's return, would be the price of my life! But—

"In order that these things may be fulfilled," he continued, "I must permit you to return to your house. So it is written, so it shall be. Your life is in my hands; beware when it is demanded of you that you hesitate not in yielding up the key!"

He raised his hands before him, making a sort of obeisance, I doubt not in the direction of Mecca, drew aside one of the yellow hangings behind him and disappeared, leaving me alone again in that nightmare apartment of yellow and green and gold. A moment I stood watching the swaying curtain. Utter silence reigned, and a sort of panic seized me infinitely greater than that occasioned by the presence of the weird Sheikh. I felt that I must escape from the place or that I should become raving mad.

I leapt forward to the curtain which Hassan had raised and jerked it aside; it had concealed a door. In this door and about level with my eyes was a kind of little barred window through which shone a dim green light. I bent forward, peering into the place beyond, but was unable to perceive anything save a vague greenness.

And as I peered, half believing that the whole episode was a dreadful, fevered dream, the abominable fumes of hashish grew, or seemed to grow, quite suddenly insupportable. Through the square opening, from the green void beyond, a cloud of oily vapour, pungent, stifling, resembling that of burning Indian hemp, poured out and enveloped me!

With a gasping cry I fell back, fighting for breath, for a breath of clean air unpolluted with hashish. But every inhalation drew down into my lungs the fumes that I sought to escape from. I experienced a deathly sickness; I seemed to be sinking into a sea of hashish, amid bubbles of yellow and green and gold, and I knew no more until, struggling again to my feet, surrounded by utter darkness—I struck my head on the corner of my writing-table ... for I lay in my own study!

My revolver, unloaded, was upon the table beside me. The night was very still. I think it must have been near to dawn.

"My God!" I whispered, "did I dream it all? Did I dream it all?"

CHAPTER XXI
THE BLACK TUBE

"There's no doubt in my mind," said Inspector Bristol, "that your experience was real enough."

The sun was shining into my room now, but could not wholly disperse the cloud of horror which lay upon it. That I had been drugged was sufficiently evident from my present condition, and that I had been taken away from my chambers Inspector Bristol had satisfactorily proved by an examination of the soles of my slippers.

"It was a clever trick," he said. "God knows what it was they puffed into your face through the letter box, but the devilish arts of ten centuries, we must remember, are at the command of Hassan of Aleppo! The repetition of the trick at the mysterious place you were taken to is particularly interesting. I should say you won't be in a hurry to peer through letter boxes and so forth in the future?"

I shook my aching head.

"That accursed yellow room," I replied, "stank with the fumes of hashish. It may have been some preparation of hashish that was used to drug me."

Bristol stood looking thoughtfully from the window.

"It was a nightmare business, Mr. Cavanagh," he said; "but it doesn't advance our inquiry a little bit. The prophecy of the old man with the white beard—whom you assure me to be none other than Hassan of Aleppo—is something we cannot very well act upon. He clearly believes it himself; for he has released you after having captured you, evidently in order that you may be at liberty to take up your duty as trustee of the slipper again. If the slipper really comes back to the Museum the fact will show Hassan to be something little short of a magician. I shan't envy you then, Mr. Cavanagh, considering that you hold the keys of the case!"

"No," I replied wearily. "Poor Professor Deeping thought that he acted in my interests and that my possession of the keys would constitute a safeguard. He was wrong. It has plunged me into the very vortex of this ghastly affair."

"It is maddening," said Bristol, "to know that Hassan and Company are snugly located somewhere under our very noses, and that all Scotland Yard can find no trace of them. Then to think that Hassan of Aleppo, apparently by means of some mystical light, has knowledge of the whereabouts of the slipper and consequently of the whereabouts of Earl Dexter (another badly wanted man) is extremely discouraging! I feel like an amateur; I'm ashamed of myself!"

Bristol departed in a condition of irritable uncertainty.

My head in my hands, I sat for long after his departure, with the phantom characters of the ghoulish drama dancing through my brain. The distorted yellow dwarfs seemed to gibe apish before me. Severed hands clenched and unclenched themselves in my face, and gleaming knives flashed across the mental picture. Predominant over all was the stately figure of Hassan of Aleppo, that benignant, remorseless being, that terrible guardian of the holy relic who directed the murderous operations. Earl Dexter, The Stetson Man, with his tightly bandaged arm, his gaunt, clean-shaven face and daredevil smile, figured, too, in my feverish daydream; nor was that other character missing, the girl with the violet eyes whose beautiful presence I had come to dread; for like a sybil announcing destruction her appearances in the drama had almost invariably presaged fresh tragedies. I recalled my previous meetings with this woman of mystery. I recalled my many surmises regarding her real identity and association with the case. I wondered why in the not very distant past I had promised to keep silent respecting her; I wondered why up to that present moment, knowing beyond doubt that her activities were inimical to my interests, were criminal, I had observed that foolish pledge.

And now my door-bell was ringing—as intuitively I had anticipated. So certain was I of the identity of my visitor that as I walked along the passage I was endeavouring to make up my mind how I should act, how I should receive her.

I opened the door; and there, wearing European garments but a green turban ... stood Hassan of Aleppo!

When I say that amazement robbed me of the power to speak, to move, almost to think, I doubt not you will credit me. Indeed, I felt that modern London was crumbling about me and that I was become involved in the fantastic mazes of one of those Oriental intrigues such as figure in the Romance of Abu Zeyd, or with which most European readers have been rendered familiar by the glowing pages of "The Thousand and One Nights."

"Effendim," said my visitor, "do not hesitate to act as I direct!"

In his gloved hand he carried what appeared to be an ebony cane. He raised and pointed it directly at me. I perceived that it was, in fact, a hollow tube.

"Death is in my hand," he continued; "enter slowly and I will follow you."

Still the sense of unreality held me thralled and my brain refused me service. Like an hypnotic subject I walked back to my study, followed by my terrible visitor, who reclosed the door behind him.

He sat facing me across my littered table with the mysterious tube held loosely in his grasp.

How infinitely more terrifying are perils unknown than those known and appreciated! Had a European armed with a pistol attempted a similar act of coercion, I cannot doubt that I should have put up some sort of fight; had he sat before me now as Hassan of Aleppo sat, with a comprehensible weapon thus laid upon his knees, I should have taken my chance, should have attacked him with the lamp, with a chair, with anything that came to my hand.

But before this awful, mysterious being who was turning my life into channels unsuspected, before that black tube with its unknown potentialities, I sat in a kind of passive panic which I cannot attempt to describe, which I had never experienced before and have never known since.

"There is one about to visit you," he said, "whom you know, whom I think you expect. For it is written that she shall come and such events cast a shadow before them. I, too, shall be present at your meeting!"

His eagle eyes opened widely; they burned with fanaticism.

"Already she is here!" he resumed suddenly, and bent as one listening. "She comes under the archway; she crossed the courtyard—and is upon the stair! Admit her, effendim; I shall be close behind you!"

The door-bell rang.

With the consciousness that the black tube was directed toward the back of my head, I went and opened the door. My mind was at work again, and busy with plans to terminate this impossible situation.

On the landing stood a girl wearing a simple white frock which fitted her graceful figure perfectly. A white straw hat, of the New York tourist type, with a long veil draped from the back suited her delicate beauty very well. The red mouth drooped a little at the corners, but the big violet eyes, like lamps of the soul, seemed afire with mystic light.

"Mr. Cavanagh," she said, very calmly and deliberately, "there is only one way now to end all this trouble. I come from the man who can return the slipper to where it belongs; but he wants his price!"

Her quiet speech served completely to restore my mental balance, and I noted with admiration that her words were so chosen as to commit her in no way. She knew quite well that thus far she might appear in the matter with impunity, and she clearly was determined to say nothing that could imperil her.

"Will you please come in?" I said quietly—and stood aside to admit her.

Exhibiting wonderful composure, she entered—and there, in the badly lighted hallway came face to face with my other visitor!

It was a situation so dramatic as to seem unreal.

Away from that tall figure retreated the girl with the violet eyes—and away—until she stood with her back to the wall. Even in the gloom I could see that her composure was deserting her; her beautiful face was pallid.

"Oh, God!" she whispered, all but inaudible—"You!"

Hassan, grasping the black rod in his hand, signed to her to enter the study. She stood quite near to me, with her eyes fixed upon him. I bent closer to her.

"My revolver—in left-hand table drawer," I breathed in her ear. "Get it. He is watching me!"

I could not tell if my words had been understood, for, never taking her gaze from the Sheikh of the Assassins, she sidled into the study. I followed her; and Hassan came last of all. Just within the doorway he stood, confronting us.

"You have come," he said, addressing the girl and speaking in perfect English but with a marked accent, "to open your impudent negotiations through Mr. Cavanagh for the return of the thrice holy relic to the Museum! Your companion, the man, who is inspired by the Evil One, has even dared to demand ransom for the slipper from me!"

Hassan was majestic in his wrath; but his eyes were black with venomous hatred.

"He has suffered the penalty which the Koran lays down; he has lost his right hand. But the lord of all evil protects him, else ere this he had lost his life! Move no closer to that table!"

I started. Either Hassan of Aleppo was omniscient or he had overheard my whispered words!

"Easily I could slay you where you stand!" he continued. "But to do so would profit me nothing. This meeting has been revealed to me. Last night I witnessed it as I slept. Also it has been revealed to me by Erroohanee, in the mirror of ink, that the slipper of the Prophet, Salla-'llahu 'ale yhi wasellem! Shall indeed return to that place accursed, that infidel eyes may look upon it! It is the will of Allah, whose name be exalted, that I hold my hand, but it is also His will that I be here, at whatever danger to my worthless body."

He turned his blazing eyes upon me.

"To-morrow, ere noon," he said, "the slipper will again be in the Museum from which the man of evil stole it. So it is written; obscure are the ways. We met last night, you and I, but at that time much was dark to me that now is light. The holy 'Alee spoke to me in a vision, saying: 'There are two keys to the case in which it will be locked. Secure one, leaving the other with him who holds it! Let him swear to be secret. This shall be the price of his life!'"

The black tube was pointed directly at my forehead.

"Effendim," concluded the speaker, "place in my hand the key of the case in the Antiquarian Museum!"

Hands convulsively clenched, the girl was looking from me to Hassan. My throat felt parched, but I forced speech to my lips.

"Your omniscience fails you," I said. "Both keys are at my bank!"

Blacker grew the fierce eyes—and blacker. I gave myself up for lost; I awaited death—death by some awful, unique means—with what courage I could muster.

From the court below came the sound of voices, the voices of passers-by who so little suspected what was happening near to them that had someone told them they certainly had refused to credit it. The noise of busy Fleet Street came drumming under the archway, too.

Then, above all, another sound became audible. To this day I find myself unable to define it; but it resembled the note of a silver bell.

Clearly it was a signal; for, hearing it, Hassan dropped the tube and glanced toward the open window.

In that instant I sprang upon him!

That I had to deal with a fanatic, a dangerous madman, I knew; that it was his life or mine, I was fully convinced. I struck out then and caught him fairly over the heart. He reeled back, and I made a wild clutch for the damnable tube, horrid, unreasoning fear of which thus far had held me inert.

I heard the girl scream affrightedly, and I knew, and felt my heart chill to know, that the tube had been wrenched from my hand! Hassan of Aleppo, old man that he appeared, had the strength of a tiger. He recovered himself and hurled me from him so that I came to the floor crashingly half under my writing-table!

Something he cried back at me, furiously—and like an enraged animal, his teeth gleaming out from his beard, he darted from the room. The front door banged loudly.

Shaken and quivering, I got upon my feet. On the threshold, in a state of pitiable hesitancy, stood the pale, beautiful accomplice of Earl Dexter. One quick glance she flashed at me, then turned and ran!

Again the door slammed. I ran to the window, looking out into the court. The girl came hurrying down the steps, and with never a backward glance ran on and was lost to view in one of the passages opening riverward.

Out under the arch, statelily passed a tall figure—and Inspector Bristol was entering! I saw the detective glance aside as the two all but met. He stood still, and looked back!

"Bristol!" I cried, and waved my arms frantically.

"Stop him! Stop him! It's Hassan of Aleppo!"

Bristol was not the only one to hear my wild cry—not the only one to dash back under the arch and out into Fleet Street.

But Hassan of Aleppo was gone!

CHAPTER XXII
THE LIGHT OF EL-MEDINEH

Bristol and I walked slowly in the direction of the entrance of the British Antiquarian Museum. It was the day following upon the sensational scene in my chambers.

"There's very little doubt," said Bristol, "that Earl Dexter has the slipper and that Hassan of Aleppo knows where Dexter is in hiding. I don't know which of the two is more elusive. Hassan apparently melted into thin air yesterday; and although The Stetson Man has never within my experience employed disguises, no one has set eyes upon him since the night that he vanished from his lodgings off the Waterloo Road. It's always possible for a man to baffle the police by remaining closely within doors, but during all the time that has elapsed Dexter must have taken a little exercise occasionally, and the missing hand should have betrayed him."

"The wonder to me is," I replied, "that he has escaped death at the hands of the Hashishin. He is a supremely daring man, for I should think that he must be carrying the slipper of the Prophet about with him!"

"I would rather he did it than I!" commented Bristol. "For sheer audacity commend me to The Stetson Man! His idea no doubt was to use you as intermediary in his negotiations with the Museum authorities, but that plan failing, he has written them direct, thoughtfully omitting his address, of course!"

We were, in fact, at that moment bound for the Museum to inspect this latest piece of evidence.

"The crowning example of the man's audacity and cleverness," added my companion, "is his having actually approached Hassan of Aleppo with a similar proposition! How did he get in touch with him? All Scotland Yard has failed to find any trace of that weird character!"

"Birds of a feather—" I suggested.

"But they are not birds of a feather!" cried Bristol. "On your own showing, Hassan of Aleppo is simply waiting his opportunity to balance Dexter's account forever! I always knew Dexter was a clever man; I begin to think he's the most daring genius alive!"

We mounted the steps of the Museum. In the hallway Mostyn, the curator, awaited us. Having greeted Bristol and myself he led the way to his private office, and from a pigeon-hole in his desk took out a letter typewritten upon a sheet of quarto paper.

Bristol spread it out upon the blotting pad and we bent over it curiously.

SIR—

I believe I can supply information concerning the whereabouts of the missing slipper of Mohammed. As any inquiry of this nature must be extremely perilous to the inquirer and as the relic is a priceless one, my fee would be 10,000 pounds. The fanatics who seek to restore the slipper to the East must not know of any negotiations, therefore I omit my address, but will communicate further if you care to insert instructions in the agony column of Times.

Faithfully,
EARL DEXTER

Bristol laughed grimly.

"It's a daring game," he said; "a piece of barefaced impudence quite characteristic.

"He's posing as a sort of private detective now, and is prepared for a trifling consideration to return the slipper which he stole himself! He must know, though, that we have his severed hand at the Yard to be used in evidence against him."

"Is the Burton Room open to the public again?" I asked Mostyn.

"It is open, yes," he replied, "and a quite unusual number of visitors come daily to gaze at the empty case which once held the slipper of the Prophet."

"Has the case been mended?"

"Yes; it is quite intact again; only the exhibit is missing."

We ascended the stairs, passed along the Assyrian Room, which seemed to be unusually crowded, and entered the lofty apartment known as the Burton Room. The sunblinds were drawn, and a sort of dim, religious light prevailed therein. A group of visitors stood around an empty case at the farther end of the apartment.

"You see," said Mostyn, pointing, "that empty case has a greater attraction than all the other full ones!"

But I scarcely heeded his words, for I was intently watching the movements of one of the group about the empty case. I have said that the room was but dimly illuminated, and this fact, together no doubt with some effect of reflected light, enhanced by my imagination, perhaps produced the phenomenon which was occasioning me so much amazement.

Remember that my mind was filled with memories of weird things, that I often found myself thinking of that mystic light which Hassan of Aleppo had called the light of El-Medineh—that light whereby, undeterred by distance, he claimed to be able to trace the whereabouts of any of the relics of the Prophet.

Bristol and Mostyn walked on then; but I stood just within the doorway, intently, breathlessly watching an old man wearing an out-of-date Inverness coat and a soft felt hat. He had a gray beard and moustache, and long, untidy hair, walked with a stoop, and in short was no unusual type of Visitor to that institution.

But it seemed to me, and the closer I watched him the more convinced I became, that this was no optical illusion, that a faint luminosity, a sort of elfin light, played eerily about his head!

As Bristol and Mostyn approached the case the old man began to walk toward me and in the direction of the door. The idea flashed through my mind that it might be Hassan of Aleppo himself, Hassan who had predicted that the stolen slipper should that day be returned to the Museum!

Then he came abreast of me, passed me, and I felt that my surmise had been wrong. I saw Bristol, from farther up the room, turn and look back. Something attracted his trained eye, I suppose, which was not perceptible to me. But he suddenly came striding along. Obviously he was pursuing the old man, who was just about to leave the apartment. Seeing that the latter had reached the doorway, Bristol began to run.

The old man turned; and amid a chorus of exclamations from the astonished spectators, Bristol sprang upon him!

How it all came about I cannot say, cannot hope to describe; but there was a short, sharp scuffle, the crack of a well-directed blow ... and Bristol was rolling on his back, the old man, hatless, was racing up the Assyrian Room, and everyone in the place seemed to be shouting at once!

Bristol, with blood streaming from his face, staggered to his feet, clutching at me for support.

"After him, Mr. Cavanagh!" he cried hoarsely. "It's your turn to-day! After him! That's Earl Dexter!"

Mostyn waited for no more, but went running quickly through the Assyrian Room. I may mention here that at the head of the stairs he found the caped Inverness which had served to conceal Dexter's mutilated arm, and later, behind a piece of statuary, a wig and a very ingenious false beard and moustache were discovered. But of The Stetson Man there was no trace. His brief start had enabled him to make good his escape.

As Mostyn went off, and a group of visitors flocked in our direction, Bristol, who had been badly shaken by the blow, turned to them.

"You will please all leave the Burton Room immediately," he said.

Looks of surprise greeted his words; but with his handkerchief raised to his face, he peremptorily repeated them. The official note in his voice was readily to be detected; and the wonder-stricken group departed with many a backward glance.

As the last left the Burton Room, Bristol pointed, with a rather shaky finger, at the soft felt hat which lay at his feet. It had formed part of Dexter's disguise. Close beside it lay another object which had evidently fallen from the hat—a dull red thing lying on the polished parquet flooring.

"For God's sake don't go near it!" whispered Bristol. "The room must be closed for the present. And now I'm off after that man. Step clear of it."

His words were unnecessary; I shunned it as a leprous thing.

It was the slipper of the Prophet!

CHAPTER XXIII
THE THREE MESSAGES

I stood in the foyer of the Astoria Hotel. About me was the pulsing stir of transatlantic life, for the tourist season was now at its height, and I counted myself fortunate in that I had been able to secure a room at this establishment, always so popular with American visitors. Chatting groups surrounded me and I became acquainted with numberless projects for visiting the Tower of London, the National Gallery, the British Museum, Windsor Castle, Kew Gardens, and the other sights dear to the heart of our visiting cousins. Loaded lifts ascended and descended. Bradshaws were in great evidence everywhere; all was hustle and glad animation.

The tall military-looking man who stood beside me glanced about him with a rather grim smile.

"You ought to be safe enough here, Mr. Cavanagh!" he said.

"I ought to be safe enough in my own chambers," I replied wearily. "How many of these pleasure-seeking folk would believe that a man can be as greatly in peril of his life in Fleet Street as in the most uncivilized spot upon the world map? Do you think if I told that prosperous New Yorker who is buying a cigar yonder, for instance, that I had been driven from my chambers by a band of Eastern assassins founded some time in the eleventh century, he would believe it?"

"I am certain he wouldn't!" replied Bristol. "I should not have credited it myself before I was put in charge of this damnable case."

My position at that hour was in truth an incredible one. The sacred slipper of Mohammed lay once more in the glass case at the Antiquarian Museum from which Earl Dexter had stolen it. Now, with apish yellow faces haunting my dreams, with ghostly menaces dogging me day and night, I was outcast from my own rooms and compelled, in self-defence, to live amid the bustle of the Astoria. So wholly nonplussed were the police authorities that they could afford me no protection. They knew that a group of scientific murderers lay hidden in or near to London; they knew that Earl Dexter, the foremost crook of his day, was also in the metropolis—and they could make no move, were helpless; indeed, as Bristol had confessed, were hopeless!

Bristol, on the previous day, had unearthed the Greek cigar merchant, Acepulos, who had replaced the slipper in its case (for a monetary consideration). He had performed a similar service when the bloodstained thing had first been put upon exhibition at the Museum, and for a considerable period had disappeared. We had feared that his religious pretensions had not saved him from the avenging scimitar of Hassan; but quite recently he had returned again to his Soho shop, and in time thus to earn a second cheque.

As Bristol and I stood glancing about the foyer of the hotel, a plain-clothes officer whom I knew by sight came in and approached my companion. I could not divine the fact, of course, but I was about to hear news of the money-loving and greatly daring Graeco-Moslem.

The detective whispered something to Bristol, and the latter started, and paled. He turned to me.

"They haven't overlooked him this time, Mr. Cavanagh," he said. "Acepulos has been found dead in his room, nearly decapitated!"

I shuddered involuntarily. Even there, amid the chatter and laughter of those light-hearted tourists, the shadow of Hassan of Aleppo was falling upon me.

Bristol started immediately for Soho and I parted from him in the Strand, he proceeding west and I eastward, for I had occasion that morning to call at my bank. It was the time of the year when London is full of foreigners, and as I proceeded in the direction of Fleet Street I encountered more than one Oriental. To my excited imagination they all seemed to glance at me furtively, with menacing eyes, but in any event I knew that I had little to fear whilst I contrived to keep to the crowded thoroughfares. Solitude I dreaded and with good reason.

Then at the door of the bank I found fresh matter for reflection. The assistant manager, Mr. Colby, was escorting a lady to the door. As I stood aside, he walked with her to a handsome car which waited, and handed her in with marks of great deference. She was heavily veiled and I had no more than a glimpse of her, but she appeared to be of middle age and had gray hair and a very stately manner.

I told myself that I was unduly suspicious, suspicious of everyone and of everything; yet as I entered the bank I found myself wondering where I had seen that dignified, grayhaired figure before. I even thought of asking the manager the name of his distinguished customer, but did not do so, for in the circumstances such an inquiry must have appeared impertinent.

My business transacted, I came out again by the side entrance which opens on the little courtyard, for this branch of the London County and Provincial Bank occupies a corner site.

A ragged urchin who was apparently waiting for me handed me a note. I looked at him inquiringly.

"For me?" I said.

"Yes, sir. A dark gentleman pointed you out as you was goin' into the bank."

The note was written upon a half sheet of paper and, doubting if it was really intended for me, I unfolded it and read the following—

Mr. Cavanagh, take the keys of the case containing the holy slipper to your hotel this evening without fail.
HASSAN.

"Who gave you this, boy?" I asked sharply.

"A foreign gentleman, sir, very dark—like an Indian."

"Where is he?"

"He went off in a cab, sir, after he give me the note."

I handed the boy sixpence and slowly pursued my way. An idea was forming in my mind to trap the enemy by seeming acquiescent. I wondered if my movements were being watched at that moment. Since it was more than probable, I returned to the bank, entered, and made some trivial inquiry of a cashier, and then came out again and walked on as far as the Report office.

I had not been in the office more than five minutes before I received a telegram from Inspector Bristol. It had been handed in at Soho, and the message was an odd one.

CAVANAGH, Report, London.
Plot afoot to steal keys. Get them from bank and join me 11 o'clock at Astoria. Have planned trap.

BRISTOL.

This was very mysterious in view of the note so recently received by me, but I concluded that Bristol had hit upon a similar plan to that which was forming in my own mind. It seemed unnecessarily hazardous, though, actually to withdraw the keys from their place of safety.

Pondering deeply upon the perplexities of this maddening case, I shortly afterward found myself again at the bank. With the manager I descended to the strong-room, and the safe was unlocked which contained the much-sought-for keys of the case at the Antiquarian Museum.

"There are the keys, quite safe!—and by the way, this is my second visit here this morning, Mr. Cavanagh," said the manager, with whom I was upon rather intimate terms. "A foreign lady who has recently become a customer of the bank deposited some valuable jewels here this morning—less than an hour ago, in fact."

"Indeed," I said, and my mind was working rapidly. "The lady who came in the large blue car, a gray-haired lady?"

"Yes," was the reply, "did you notice her, then?"

I nodded and said no more, for in truth I had no more to say. I had good reason to respect the uncanny powers of Hassan of Aleppo, but I doubted if even his omniscience could tell him (since I had actually gone down into the strong-room) whether when I emerged I had the keys, or whether my visit and seeming acceptance of his orders had been no more than a subterfuge!

That the Hashishin had some means of communicating with me at the Astoria was evident from the contents of the note which I had received, and as I walked in the direction of the hotel my mind was filled with all sorts of misgivings. I was playing with fire! Had I done rightly or should I have acted otherwise? I sighed wearily. The dark future would resolve all my doubts.

When I reached the Astoria, Bristol had not arrived. I lighted a cigarette and sat down in the lounge to await his coming. Presently a boy approached, handing me a message which had been taken down from the telephone by the clerk. It was as follows—

Tell Mr. Cavanagh, who is waiting in the hotel, to take what I am expecting to his chambers, and say that I will join him there in twenty minutes.

INSPECTOR BRISTOL.

Again I doubted the wisdom of Bristol's plan. Had I not fled to the Astoria to escape from the dangerous solitude of my rooms? That he was laying some trap for the Hashishin was sufficiently evident, and whilst I could not justly suspect him of making a pawn of me I was quite unable to find any other explanation of this latest move.

I was torn between conflicting doubts. I glanced at my watch. Yes! There was just time for me to revisit the bank ere joining Bristol at my chambers! I hesitated. After all, in what possible way could it jeopardize his plans for me merely to pretend to bring the keys?

"Hang it all!" I said, and jumped to my feet. "These maddening conjectures will turn my brain! I'll let matters stand as they are, and risk the consequences!"

I hesitated no longer, but passed out from the hotel and once more directed my steps in the direction of Fleet Street.

As I passed in under the arch through which streamed many busy workers, I told myself that to dread entering my own chambers at high noon was utterly childish. Yet I did dread doing so! And as I mounted the stair and came to the landing, which was always more or less dark, I paused for quite a long time before putting the key in the lock.

The affair of the accursed slipper was playing havoc with my nerves, and I laughed dryly to note that my hand was not quite steady as I turned the key, opened my door, and slipped into the dim hallway.

As I closed it behind me, something, probably a slight noise, but possibly something more subtle—an instinct—made me turn rapidly.

There facing me stood Hassan of Aleppo.

CHAPTER XXIV
I KEEP THE APPOINTMENT

That moment was pungent with drama. In the intense hush of the next five seconds I could fancy that the world had slipped away from me and that I was become an unsubstantial thing of dreams. I was in no sense master of myself; the effect of the presence of this white-bearded fanatic was of a kind which I am entirely unable to describe. About Hassan of Aleppo was an aroma of evil, yet of majesty, which marked him strangely different from other men—from any other that I have ever known. In his venerable presence, remembering how he was Sheikh of the Assassins, and recalling his bloody history, I was always conscious of a weakness, physical and mental. He appalled me; and now, with my back to the door, I stood watching him and watching the ominous black tube which he held in his hand. It was a weapon unknown to Europe and therefore more fearful than the most up-to-date of death-dealing instruments.

Hassan of Aleppo pointed it toward me.

"The keys, effendim," he said; "hand me the keys!"

He advanced a step; his manner was imperious. The black tube was less than a foot removed from my face. That I had my revolver in my pocket could avail me nothing, for in my pocket it must remain, since I dared to make no move to reach it under cover of that unfamiliar, terrible weapon.

The black eyes of Hassan glared insanely into mine.

"You will have placed them in your pocketcase," he said. "Take it out; hand it to me!"

I obeyed, for what else could I do? Taking the case from my pocket, I placed it in his lean brown hand.

An expression of wild exultation crossed his features; the eagle eyes seemed to be burning into my brain. A puff of hot vapour struck me in the face—something which was expelled from the mysterious black tube. And with memories crowding to my mind of similar experiences at the hands of the Hashishin, I fell back, clutching at my throat, fighting for my life against the deadly, vaporous thing that like a palpable cloud surrounded me. I tried to cry out, but the words died upon my tongue. Hassan of Aleppo seemed to grow huge before my eyes like some ginn of Eastern lore. Then a curtain of darkness descended. I experienced a violent blow upon the forehead (I suppose I had pitched forward), and for the time resigned my part in the drama of the sacred slipper.

CHAPTER XXV
THE WATCHER IN BANK CHAMBERS

At about five o'clock that afternoon Inspector Bristol, who had spent several hours in Soho upon the scene of the murder of the Greek, was walking along Fleet Street, bound for the offices of the Report. As he passed the court, on the corner of which stands a branch of the London County and Provincial Bank, his eye was attracted by a curious phenomenon.

There are reflectors above the bank windows which face the court, and it appeared to Bristol that there was a hole in one of these, the furthermost from the corner. A tiny beam of light shone from the bank window on to the reflector, or from the reflector on to the window, which circumstance in itself was not curious. But above the reflector, at an acute angle, this mysterious beam was seemingly projected upward. Walking a little way up the court he saw that it shone through, and cast a disc of light upon the ceiling of an office on the first floor of Bank Chambers above.

It is every detective's business to be observant, and although many thousands of passersby must have cast their eyes in the same direction that day, there is small matter for wonder in the fact that Bristol alone took the trouble to inquire into the mystery—for his trained eye told him that there was a mystery here.

Possibly he was in that passive frame of mind when the brain is particularly receptive of trivial impressions; for after a futile search of the Soho cigar store for anything resembling a clue, he was quite resigned to the idea of failure in the case of Hassan and Company. He walked down the court and into the entrance of Bank Chambers. An Inspection of the board upon the wall showed him that the first floor apparently was occupied by three firms, two of them legal, for this is the neighbourhood of the law courts, and the third a press agency. He stepped up to the first floor. Past the doors bearing the names of the solicitors and past that belonging to the press agent he proceeded to a fourth suite of offices. Here, pinned upon the door frame, appeared a card which bore the legend—

THE CONGO FIBRE COMPANY

Evidently the Congo Fibre Company had so recently taken possession of the offices that there had been no time to inscribe their title either upon the doors or upon the board in the hall.

Inspector Bristol was much impressed, for into one of the rooms occupied by the Fibre Company shone that curious disc of light which first had drawn his attention to Bank Chambers. He rapped on the door, turned the handle, and entered. The sole furniture of the office in which he found himself apparently consisted of one desk and an office stool, which stool was occupied by an office boy. The windows opened on the court, and a door marked "Private" evidently communicated with an inner office whose windows likewise must open on the court. It was the ceiling of this inner office, unless the detective's calculation erred, which he was anxious to inspect.

"Yes, sir?" said the boy tentatively.

Bristol produced a card which bore the uncompromising legend: John Henry Smith.

"Take my card to Mr. Boulter, boy," he said tersely. The boy stared.

"Mr. Boulter, sir? There isn't any one of that name here."

"Oh!" said Bristol, looking around him in apparent surprise: "how long is he gone?"

"I don't know, sir. I've only been here three weeks, and Mr. Knowlson only took the offices a month ago."

"Oh," commented Bristol, "then take my card to Mr. Knowlson; he will probably be able to give me Mr. Boulter's present address."

The boy hesitated. The detective had that authoritative manner which awes the youthful mind.

"He's out, sir," he said, but without conviction.

"Is he?" rapped Bristol. "Well, I'll leave my card."

He turned and quitted the office, carefully closing the door behind him. Three seconds later he reopened it, and peering in, was in time to see the boy knock upon the private door. A little wicket, or movable panel, was let down, the card of John Henry Smith was passed through to someone unseen, and the wicket was reclosed!

The boy turned and met the wrathful eye of the detective. Bristol reentered, closing the door behind him.

"See here, young fellow," said he, "I don't stand for those tricks! Why didn't you tell me Mr. Knowlson was in?"

"I'm very sorry, sir!"—the boy quailed beneath his glance—"but he won't see any one who hasn't an appointment."

"Is there someone with him, then?"

"No."

"Well, what's he doing?"

"I don't know, sir; I've never been in to see!"

"What! never been in that room?"

"Never!" declared the boy solemnly. "And I don't mind telling you," he added, recovering something of his natural confidence, "that I am leaving on the 31st. This job ain't any use to me!"

"Too much work?" suggested Bristol.

"No work at all!" returned the boy indignantly. "I'm just here for a blessed buffer, that's what I'm here for, a buffer!"

"What do you mean?"

"I just have to sit here and see that nobody gets into that office. Lively, ain't it? Where's the prospects?"

Bristol surveyed him thoughtfully.

"Look here, my lad," he said quietly; "is that door locked?"

"Always," replied the boy.

"Does Mr. Knowlson come to that shutter when you knock?"

"Yes."

"Then go and knock!"

The boy obeyed with alacrity. He rapped loudly on the door, not noticing or not caring that the visitor was standing directly behind him. The shutter was lowered and a grizzled, bearded face showed for a moment through the opening.

Bristol leant over the boy and pushed a card through into the hand of the man beyond. On this occasion it did not bear the legend "John Henry Smith," but the following—

CHIEF INSPECTOR BRISTOL
C.I.D.
NEW SCOTLAND YARD

"Good afternoon, Mr. Knowlson," said the detective dryly. "I want to come in!"

There followed a moment of silence, from which Bristol divined that he had blundered upon some mystery, possibly upon a big case; then a key was turned in the lock and the door thrown open.

"Come right in, Inspector," invited a strident voice. "Carter, you can go home."

Bristol entered warily, but not warily enough. For as the door was banged upon his entrance he faced around only in time to find himself looking down the barrel of a Colt automatic.

With his back to the door which contained the wicket, now reclosed, stood the man with the bearded face. The revolver was held in his left hand; his right arm terminated in a bandaged stump. But without that his steel-gray eyes would have betrayed him to the detective.

"Good God!" whispered Bristol. "It's Earl Dexter!"

"It is!" replied the cracksman, "and you've looked in at a real inconvenient time! My visitors mostly seem to have that knack. I'll have to ask you to stay, Inspector. Sit down in that chair yonder."

Bristol knew his man too well to think of opening any argument at that time. He sat down as directed, and ignoring the revolver which covered him all the time, began coolly to survey the room in which he found himself. In several respects it was an extraordinary apartment.

The only bright patch in the room was the shining disc upon the ceiling; and the detective noted with interest that this marked the position of an arrangement of mirrors. A white-covered table, entirely bare, stood upon the floor immediately beneath this mysterious apparatus. With the exception of one or two ordinary items of furniture and a small hand lathe, the office otherwise was unfurnished. Bristol turned his eyes again upon the daring man who so audaciously had trapped him—the man who had stolen the slipper of the Prophet and suffered the loss of his hand by the scimitar of an Hashishin as a result. When he had least expected to find one, Fate had thrown a clue in Bristol's way. He reflected grimly that it was like to prove of little use to him.

"Now," said Dexter, "you can do as you please, of course, but you know me pretty well and I advise you to sit quiet."

"I am sitting quiet!" was the reply.

"I am sorry," continued Dexter, with a quick glance at his maimed arm, "that I can't tie you up, but I am expecting a friend any moment now."

He suddenly raised the wicket with a twitch of his elbow and, without removing his gaze from the watchful detective, cried sharply—

"Carter!"

But there was no reply.

"Good; he's gone!"

Dexter sat down facing Bristol.

"I have lost my hand in this game, Mr. Bristol," he said genially, "and had some narrow squeaks of losing my head; but having gone so far and lost so much I'm going through, if I don't meet a funeral! You see I'm up against two tough propositions."

Bristol nodded sympathetically.

"The first," continued Dexter, "is you and Cavanagh, and English law generally. My idea—if I can get hold of the slipper again—oh! you needn't stare; I'm out for it!—is to get the Antiquarian Institution to ransom it. It's a line of commercial speculation I have worked successfully before. There's a dozen rich highbrows, cranks to a man, connected with it, and they are my likeliest buyers—sure. But to keep the tone of the market healthy there's Hassan of Aleppo, rot him! He's a dangerous customer to approach, but you'll note I've been in negotiation with him already and am still, if not booming, not much below par!"

"Quite so," said Bristol. "But you've cut off a pretty hefty chew nevertheless. They used to call you The Stetson Man, you used to dress like a fashion plate and stop at the big hotels. Those days are past, Dexter, I'm sorry to note. You're down to the skulking game now and you're nearer an advert for Clarkson than Stein-Bloch!"

"Yep," said Dexter sadly, "I plead guilty, but I think here's Carneta!"

Bristol heard the door of the outer office open, and a moment later that upon which his gaze was set opened in turn, to admit a girl who was heavily veiled, and who started and stood still in the doorway, on perceiving the situation. Never for one unguarded moment did the American glance aside from his prisoner.

"The Inspector's dropped in, Carneta!" he drawled in his strident way. "You're handy with a ball of twine; see if you can induce him to stay the night!"

The girl, immediately recovering her composure, took off her hat in a businesslike way and began to look around her, evidently in search of a suitable length of rope with which to fasten up Bristol.

"Might I suggest," said the detective, "that if you are shortly quitting these offices a couple of the window-cords neatly joined would serve admirably?"

"Thanks," drawled Dexter, nodding to his companion, who went into the outer office, where she might be heard lowering the windows. She was gone but a few moments ere she returned again, carrying a length of knotted rope. Under cover of Dexter's revolver, Bristol stoically submitted to having his wrists tied behind him. The end of the line was then thrown through the ventilator above the door which communicated with the outer office and Bristol was triced up in such a way that, his wrists being raised behind him to an uncomfortable degree, he was almost forced to stand upon tiptoe. The line was then secured.

"Very workmanlike!" commented the victim. "You'll find a large handkerchief in my inside breast pocket. It's a clean one, and I can recommend it as a gag!"

Very promptly it was employed for the purpose, and Inspector Bristol found himself helpless and constrained in a very painful position. Dexter laid down his revolver.

"We will now give you a free show, Inspector," he said, genially, "of our camera obscura!"

He pulled down the blinds, which Bristol noted with interest to be black, but through an opening in one of them a mysterious ray of light—the same that he had noticed from Fleet Street—shone upon that point in the ceiling where the arrangement of mirrors was attached. Dexter made some alteration, apparently in the focus of the lens (for Bristol had divined that in some way a lens had been fixed in the reflector above the bank window below) and the disc of light became concentrated. The white-covered table was moved slightly, and in the darkness some further manipulation was performed.

"Observe," came the strident voice—"we now have upon the screen here a minute moving picture. This little device, which is not protected in any way, is of my own invention, and proved extremely useful in the Arkwright jewel case, which startled Chicago. It has proved useful now. I know almost as much concerning the arrangements below as the manager himself. In confidence, Inspector, this is my last bid for the slipper! I have plunged on it. Madame Sforza, the distinguished Italian lady who recently opened an account below, opened it for 500 pounds cash. She has drawn a portion, but a balance remains which I am resigned to lose. Her motor-car (hired), her references (forged), the case of jewels which she deposited this morning (duds!)—all represent a considerable outlay. It's a nerve-racking line of operation, too. Any hour of the day may bring such a visitor as yourself, for example. In short, I am at the end of my tether."

Bristol, ignoring the increasing pain in his arms and wrists, turned his eyes upon the white-covered table and there saw a minute and clear-cut picture, such as one sees in a focussing screen, of the interior of the manager's office of the London County and Provincial Bank!

CHAPTER XXVI
THE STRONG-ROOM

I wonder how often a sense of humour has saved a man from desperation? Perhaps only the Easterns have thoroughly appreciated that divine gift. I have interpolated the adventure of Inspector Bristol in order that the sequence of my story be not broken; actually I did not learn it until later, but when, on the following day, the whole of the facts came into my possession, I laughed and was glad that I could laugh, for laughter has saved many a man from madness.

Certainly the Fates were playing with us, for at a time very nearly corresponding with that when Bristol found himself bound and helpless in Bank Chambers I awoke to find myself tied hand and foot to my own bed! Nothing but the haziest recollections came to me at first, nothing but dim memories of the awful being who had lured me there; for I perceived now that all the messages proceeded, not from Bristol, but from Hassan of Aleppo! I had been a fool, and I was reaping the fruits of my folly. Could I have known that almost within pistol shot of me the Inspector was trussed up as helpless as I, then indeed my situation must have become unbearable, since upon him I relied for my speedy release.

My ankles were firmly lashed to the rails at the foot of my bed; each of my wrists was tied back to a bedpost. I ached in every limb and my head burned feverishly, which latter symptom I ascribed to the powerful drug which had been expelled into my face by the uncanny weapon carried by Hassan of Aleppo. I reflected bitterly how, having transferred my quarters to the Astoria, I could not well hope for any visitor to my chambers; and even the event of such a visitor had been foreseen and provided against by the cunning lord of the Hashishin. A gag, of the type which Dumas has described in "Twenty Years After," the poire d'angoisse, was wedged firmly into my mouth, so that only by preserving the utmost composure could I breathe. I was bathed in cold perspiration. So I lay listening to the familiar sounds without and reflecting that it was quite possible so to lie, undisturbed, and to die alone, my presence there wholly unsuspected!

Once, toward dusk, my phone bell rang, and my state of mind became agonizing. It was maddening to think that someone, a friend, was virtually within reach of me, yet actually as far removed as if an ocean divided us! I tasted the hellish torments of Tantalus. I cursed fate, heaven, everything; I prayed; I sank into bottomless depths of despair and rose to dizzy pinnacles of hope, when a footstep sounded on the landing and a thousand wild possibilities, vague possibilities of rescue, poured into my mind.

The visitor hesitated, apparently outside my door; and a change, as sudden as lightning out of a cloud, transformed my errant fancies. A gruesome conviction seized me, as irrational as the hope which it displayed, that this was one of the Hashishin—an apish yellow dwarf, a strangler, the awful Hassan himself!

The footsteps receded down the stairs. And my thoughts reverted into the old channels of dull despair.

I weighed the chances of Bristol's seeking me there; and, eager as I was to give them substance, found them but airy—ultimately was forced to admit them to be nil.

So I lay, whilst only a few hundred yards from me a singular scene was being enacted. Bristol, a prisoner as helpless as myself, watched the concluding business of the day being conducted in the bank beneath him; he watched the lift descend to the strongroom—the spying apparatus being slightly adjusted in some way; he saw the clerks hastening to finish their work in the outer office, and as he watched, absorbed by the novelty of the situation, he almost forgot the pain and discomfort which he suffered...

"This little peep-show of ours has been real useful," Dexter confided out of the darkness. "I got an impression of the key of the strongroom door a week ago, and Carneta got one of the keys of the safe only this morning, when she lodged her box of jewellery with the bank! I was at work on that key when you interrupted me, and as by means of this useful apparatus I have learnt the combination, you ought to see some fun in the next few hours!"

Bristol repressed a groan, for the prospect of remaining in that position was thus brought keenly home to him.

The bank staff left the premises one by one until only a solitary clerk worked on at a back desk. His task completed, he, too, took his departure and the bank messenger commenced his nightly duty of sweeping up the offices.

It was then that excitement like an anaesthetic dulled the detective's pain—indeed, he forgot his aching body and became merely a watchful intelligence.

So intent had he become upon the picture before him that he had not noticed the fact that he was alone in the office of the Congo Fibre Company. Now he realized it from the absolute silence about him, and from another circumstance.

The spying apparatus had been left focussed, and on to the screen beneath his eyes, bending low behind the desks and creeping, Indian-like, around, toward the head of the stair which communicated with the strongroom and the apartment used by the messenger, came the alert figure of Earl Dexter!

It may be a surprise to some people to learn that at any time in the day the door of a bank, unguarded, should be left open, when only a solitary messenger is within the premises; yet for a few minutes at least each evening this happens at more than one City bank, where one of the duties of the resident messenger is to clean the outer steps. Dexter had taken advantage of the man's absence below in quest of scrubbing material to enter the bank through the open door.

Watching, breathless, and utterly forgetful of his own position, Bristol saw the messenger, all unconscious of danger, come up the stairs carrying a pail and broom. As his head reached the level of the railings The Stetson Man neatly sand-bagged him, rushed across to the outer door, and closed it!

Given duplicate keys and the private information which Dexter so ingeniously had obtained, there are many London banks vulnerable to similar attack. Certainly, bullion is rarely kept in a branch storeroom, but the detective was well aware that the keys of the case containing the slipper were kept in this particular safe!

He was convinced, and could entertain no shadowy doubt, that at last Dexter had triumphed. He wondered if it had ever hitherto fallen to the lot of a representative of the law thus to be made an accessory to a daring felony!

But human endurance has well-defined limits. The fading light rendered the ingenious picture dim and more dim. The pain occasioned by his position became agonizing, and uttering a stifled groan he ceased to take an interest in the robbery of the London County and Provincial Bank.

Fate is a comedian; and when later I learned how I had lain strapped to my bed, and, so near to me, Bristol had hung helpless as a butchered carcass in the office of the Congo Fibre Company, whilst, in our absence from the stage, the drama of the slipper marched feverish to its final curtain, I accorded Fate her well-earned applause. I laughed; not altogether mirthfully.

CHAPTER XXVII
THE SLIPPER

Someone was breaking in at the door of my chambers!

I aroused myself from a state of coma almost death-like and listened to the blows. The sun was streaming in at my windows.

A splintering crash told of a panel broken. Then a moment later I heard the grating of the lock, and a rush of footsteps along the passage.

"Try the study!" came a voice that sounded like Bristol's, save that it was strangely weak and shaky.

Almost simultaneously the Inspector himself threw open the bedroom door—and, very pale and haggard-eyed, stood there looking across at me. It was a scene unforgettable.

"Mr. Cavanagh!" he said huskily—"Mr. Cavanagh! Thank God you're alive! But"—he turned—"this way, Marden!" he cried, "Untie him quickly! I've got no strength in my arms!"

Marden, a C.I.D. man, came running, and in a minute, or less, I was sitting up gulping brandy.

"I've had the most awful experience of my life," said Bristol. "You've fared badly enough, but I've been hanging by my wrists—you know Dexter's trick!—for close upon sixteen hours! I wasn't released until Carter, an office boy, came on the scene this morning!"

Very feebly I nodded; I could not talk.

"The strong-room of your bank was rifled under my very eyes last evening!" he continued, with something of his old vigour; "and five minutes after the Antiquarian Museum was opened to the public this morning quite an unusual number of visitors appeared.

"I saw the bank manager the moment he arrived, and learned a piece of news that positively took my breath away! I was at the Museum seven minutes later and got another shock! There in the case was the red slipper!"

"Then," I whispered-"it hadn't been stolen?"

"Wrong! It had! This was a duplicate, as Mostyn, the curator, saw at a glance! Some of the early visitors—they were Easterns—had quite surrounded the case. They were watched, of course, but any number of Orientals come to see the thing; and, short of smashing the glass, which would immediately attract attention, the authorities were unprepared, of course, for any attempt. Anyway, they were tricked. Somebody opened the case. The real slipper of the Prophet is gone!"

"They told you at the bank—"

"That you had withdrawn the keys! If Dexter had known that!"

"Hassan of Aleppo took them from me last night! At last the Hashishin have triumphed."

Bristol sank into the armchair.

"Every port is watched," he said. "But—"

CHAPTER XXVIII
CARNETA

"I am entirely at your mercy; you can do as you please with me. But before you do anything I should like you to listen to what I have to say."

Her beautiful face was pale and troubled. Violet eyes looked sadly into mine.

"For nearly an hour I have been waiting for this chance—until I knew you were alone," she continued. "If you are thinking of giving me up to the police, at least remember that I came here of my own free will. Of course, I know you are quite entitled to take advantage of that; but please let me say what I came to say!"

She pleaded so hard, with that musical voice, with her evident helplessness, most of all with her wonderful eyes, that I quite abandoned any project I might have entertained to secure her arrest. I think she divined this masculine weakness, for she said, with greater confidence—

"Your friend, Professor Deeping, was murdered by the man called Hassan of Aleppo. Are you content to remain idle while his murderer escapes?"

God knows I was not. My idleness in the matter was none of my choosing. Since poor Deeping's murder I had come to handgrips with the assassins more than once, but Hassan had proved too clever for me, too clever for Scotland Yard. The sacred slipper was once more in the hands of its fanatic guardian.

One man there was who might have helped the search, Earl Dexter. But Earl Dexter was himself wanted by Scotland Yard!

From the time of the bank affair up to the moment when this beautiful visitor had come to my chambers I had thought Dexter, as well as Hassan, to have fled secretly from England. But the moment that I saw Carneta at my door I divined that The Stetson Man must still be in London.

She sat watching me and awaiting my answer.

"I cannot avenge my friend unless I can find his murderer."

Eagerly she bent forward.

"But if I can find him?"

That made me think, and I hesitated before speaking again.

"Say what you came to say," I replied slowly. "You must know that I distrust you. Indeed, my plain duty is to detain you. But I will listen to anything you may care to tell me, particularly if it enables me to trap Hassan of Aleppo."

"Very well," she said, and rested her elbows upon the table before her. "I have come to you in desperation. I can help you to find the man who murdered Professor Deeping, but in return I want you to help me!"

I watched her closely. She was very plainly, almost poorly, dressed. Her face was pale and there were dark marks around her eyes. This but served to render their strange beauty more startling; yet I could see that my visitor was in real trouble. The situation was an odd one.

"You are possibly about to ask me," I suggested, "to assist Earl Dexter to escape the police?"

She shook her head. Her voice trembled as she replied—

"That would not have induced me to run the risk of coming here. I came because I wanted to find a man who was brave enough to help me. We have no friends in London, and so it became a question of terms. I can repay you by helping you to trace Hassan."

"What is it, then, that Dexter asks me to do?"

"He asks nothing. I, Carneta, am asking!"

"Then you are not come from him?"

At my question, all her self-possession left her. She abruptly dropped her face into her hands and was shaken with sobs! It was more than I could bear, unmoved. I forgot the shady past, forgot that she was the associate of a daring felon, and could only realize that she was a weeping woman, who had appealed to my pity and who asked my aid.

I stood up and stared out of the window, for I experienced a not unnatural embarrassment. Without looking at her I said—

"Don't be afraid to tell me your troubles. I don't say I should go out of my way to be kind to Mr. Dexter, but I have no wish whatever to be instrumental in"—I hesitated—"in making you responsible for his misdeeds. If you can tell me where to find Hassan of Aleppo, I won't even ask you where Dexter is—"

"God help me! I don't know where he is!"

There was real, poignant anguish in her cry. I turned and confronted her. Her lashes were all wet with tears.

"What! has he disappeared?"

She nodded, fought with her emotion a moment, and went on unsteadily,

"I want you to help me to find him for in finding him we shall find Hassan!"

"How so?"

Her gaze avoided me now.

"Mr. Cavanagh, he has staked everything upon securing the slipper—and the Hashishin were too clever for him. His hand—those Eastern fiends cut off his hand! But he would not give in. He made another bid—and lost again. It left him almost penniless."

She spoke of Earl Dexter's felonious plans as another woman might have spoken of her husband's unwise investments! It was fantastic hearing that confession of The Stetson Man's beautiful partner, and I counted the interview one of the strangest I had ever known.

A sudden idea came to me. "When did Dexter first conceive the plan to steal the slipper?" I asked.

"In Egypt!" answered Carneta. "Yes! You may as well know! He is thoroughly familiar with the East, and he learned of the robbery of Professor Deeping almost as soon as it became known to Hassan. I know what you are going to ask—"

"Ahmad Ahmadeen!"

"Yes! He travelled home as Ahmadeen—the only time he ever used a disguise. Oh! the thing is accursed!" she cried. "I begged him, implored him, to abandon his attempts upon it. Day and night we were watched by those ghastly yellow men! But it was all in vain. He knew, had known for a long time, where Hassan of Aleppo was in hiding!"

And I reflected that the best men at New Scotland Yard had failed to pick up the slightest clue!

"The Hashishin, of whom that dreadful man is leader, are rich, or have supporters who are rich. The plan was to make them pay for the slipper."

"My God! it was playing with fire!"

She sat silent awhile. Emotion threatened to get the upper hand. Then—

"Two days ago," she almost whispered, "he set out—to ... get the slipper!"

"To steal it?"

"To steal it!"

"From Hassan of Aleppo?"

I could scarcely believe that any man, single-handed, could have had the hardihood to attempt such a thing.

"From Hassan, yes!"

I faced her, amazed, incredulous.

"Dexter had suffered mutilation, he knew that the Hashishin sought his life for his previous attempts upon the relic of the Prophet, and yet he dared to venture again into the very lions' den?"

"He did, Mr. Cavanagh, two days ago. And—"

"Yes?" I urged, as gently as I could, for she was shaking pitifully.

"He never came back!"

The words were spoken almost in a whisper. She clenched her hands and leapt from the chair, fighting down her grief and with such a stark horror in her beautiful eyes that from my very soul I longed to be able to help her.

"Mr. Cavanagh" (she had courage, this bewildering accomplice of a cracksman), "I know the house he went to! I cannot hope to make you understand what I have suffered since then. A thousand times I have been on the point of going to the police, confessing all I knew, and leading them to that house! O God! if only he is alive, this shall be his last crooked deal—and mine! I dared not go to the police, for his sake! I waited, and watched, and hoped, through two such nights and days ... then I ventured. I should have gone mad if I had not come here. I knew you had good cause to hate, to detest me, but I remembered that you had a great grievance against Hassan. Not as great, O heaven! not as great as mine, but yet a great one. I remembered, too, that you were the kind of man—a woman can come to..."

She sank back into the chair, and with her fingers twining and untwining, sat looking dully before her.

"In brief," I said, "what do you propose?"

"I propose that we endeavour to obtain admittance to the house of Hassan of Aleppo—secretly, of course, and all I ask of you in return for revealing the secret of its situation is—"

"That I let Dexter go free?"

Almost inaudibly she whispered: "If he lives!"

Surely no stranger proposition ever had been submitted to a law-abiding citizen. I was asked to connive in the escape of a notorious criminal, and at one and the same time to embark upon an expedition patently burglarious! As though this were not enough, I was invited to beard Hassan of Aleppo, the most dreadful being I had ever encountered East or West, in his mysterious stronghold!

I wondered what my friend, Inspector Bristol, would have thought of the project; I wondered if I should ever live to see Hassan meet his just deserts as a result of this enterprise, which I was forced to admit a foolhardy one. But a man who has selected the career of a war correspondent from amongst those which Fleet Street offers, is the victim of a certain craving for fresh experiences; I suppose, has in his character something of an adventurous turn.

For a while I stood staring from the window, then faced about and looked into the violet eyes of my visitor.

"I agree, Carneta!" I said.

CHAPTER XXIX
WE MEET MR. ISAACS

Quitting the wayside station, and walking down a short lane, we came out upon Watling Street, white and dusty beneath the afternoon sun. We were less than an hour's train journey from London but found ourselves amid the Kentish hop gardens, amid a rural peace unbroken. My companion carried a camera case slung across her shoulder, but its contents were less innocent than one might have supposed. In fact, it contained a neat set of those instruments of the burglar's art with whose use she appeared to be quite familiar.

"There is an inn," she said, "about a mile ahead, where we can obtain some vital information. He last wrote to me from there."

Side by side we tramped along the dusty road. We both were silent, occupied with our own thoughts. Respecting the nature of my companion's I could entertain little doubt, and my own turned upon the foolhardy nature of the undertaking upon which I was embarked. No other word passed between us then, until upon rounding a bend and passing a cluster of picturesque cottages, the yard of the Vinepole came into view.

"Do they know you by sight here?" I asked abruptly.

"No, of course not; we never made strategic mistakes of that kind. If we have tea here, no doubt we can learn all we require."

I entered the little parlour of the inn, and suggested that tea should be served in the pretty garden which opened out of it upon the right.

The host, who himself laid the table, viewed the camera case critically.

"We get a lot of photographers down here," he remarked tentatively.

"No doubt," said my companion. "There is some very pretty scenery in the neighbourhood."

The landlord rested his hands upon the table.

"There was a gentleman here on Wednesday last," he said; "an old gentleman who had met with an accident, and was staying somewhere hereabouts for his health. But he'd got his camera with him, and it was wonderful the way he could use it, considering he hadn't got the use of his right hand."

"He must have been a very keen photographer," I said, glancing at the girl beside me.

"He took three or four pictures of the Vinepole," replied the landlord (which I doubted, since probably his camera was a dummy); "and he wanted to know if there were any other old houses in the neighbourhood. I told him he ought to take Cadham Hall, and he said he had heard that the Gate House, which is about a mile from here, was one of the oldest buildings about."

A girl appeared with a tea tray, and for a moment I almost feared that the landlord was about to retire; but he lingered, whilst the girl distributed the things about the table, and Carneta asked casually, "Would there be time for me to photograph the Gate House before dark?"

"There might be time," was the reply, "but that's not the difficulty. Mr. Isaacs is the difficulty."

"Who is Mr. Isaacs?" I asked.

"He's the Jewish gentleman who bought the Gate House recently. Lots of money he's got and a big motor car. He's up and down to London almost every day in the week, but he won't let anybody take photographs of the house. I know several who've asked."

"But I thought," said Carneta, innocently, "you said the old gentleman who was here on Wednesday went to take some?"

"He went, yes, miss; but I don't know if he succeeded."

Carneta poured out some tea.

"Now that you speak of it," she said, "I too have heard that the Gate House is very picturesque. What objection can Mr. Isaacs have to photographers?"

"Well, you see, miss, to get a picture of the house, you have to pass right through the grounds."

"I should walk right up to the house and ask permission. Is Mr. Isaacs at home, I wonder?"

"I couldn't say. He hasn't passed this way to-day."

"We might meet him on the way," said I. "What is he like?"

"A Jewish gentleman sir, very dark, with a white beard. Wears gold glasses. Keeps himself very much to himself. I don't know anything about his household; none of them ever come here."

Carneta inquired the direction of Cadham Hall and of the Gate House, and the landlord left us to ourselves. My companion exhibited signs of growing agitation, and it seemed to me that she had much ado to restrain herself from setting out without a moment's delay for the Gate House, which, I readily perceived, was the place to which our strange venture was leading us.

I found something very stimulating in the reflection that, rash though the expedition might be, and, viewed from whatever standpoint, undeniably perilous, it promised to bring me to that secret stronghold of deviltry where the sinister Hassan of Aleppo so successfully had concealed himself.

The work of the modern journalist had many points of contact with that of the detective; and since the murder of Professor Deeping I had succumbed to the man-hunting fever more than once. I knew that Scotland Yard had failed to locate the hiding-place of the remarkable and evil man who, like an efreet of Oriental lore, obeyed the talisman of the stolen slipper, striking down whomsoever laid hand upon its sacredness. It was a novel sensation to know that, aided by this beautiful accomplice of a rogue, I had succeeded where the experts had failed!

Misgivings I had and shall not deny. If our scheme succeeded it would mean that Deeping's murderer should be brought to justice. If it failed-well, frankly, upon that possibility I did not dare to reflect!

It must be needless for me to say that we two strangely met allies were ill at ease, sometimes to the point of embarrassment. We proceeded on our way in almost unbroken silence, and, save for a couple of farm hands, without meeting any wayfarer, up to the time that we reached the brow of the hill and had our first sight of the Gate House lying in a little valley beneath. It was a small Tudor mansion, very compact in plan and its roof glowed redly in the rays of the now setting sun.

From the directions given by the host of the Vinepole it was impossible to mistake the way or to mistake the house. Amid well-wooded grounds it stood, a place quite isolated, but so typically English that, as I stood looking down upon it, I found myself unable to believe that any other than a substantial country gentleman could be its proprietor.

I glanced at Carneta. Her violet eyes were burning feverishly, but her lips twitched in a bravely pitiful way.

Clearly now my adventure lay before me; that red-roofed homestead seemed to have rendered it all substantial which hitherto had been shadowy; and I stood there studying the Gate House gravely, for it might yet swallow me up, as apparently it had swallowed Earl Dexter.

There, amid that peaceful Kentish landscape, fantasy danced and horrors unknown lurked in waiting...

The eminence upon which we were commanded an extensive prospect, and eastward showed a tower and flagstaff which marked the site of Cadham Hall. There were homeward-bound labourers to be seen in the lanes now, and where like a white ribbon the Watling Street lay across the verdant carpet moved an insect shape, speedily.

It was a car, and I watched it with vague interest. At a point where a dense coppice spread down to the roadway and a lane crossed west to east, the car became invisible. Then I saw it again, nearer to us and nearer to the Gate House. Finally it disappeared among the trees.

I turned to Carneta. She, too, had been watching. Now her gaze met mine.

"Mr. Isaacs!" she said; and her voice was less musical than usual. "His chauffeur, who learned his business in Cairo, is probably the only one of his servants who remains in England."

"What!" I began—and said no more.

Where the road upon which we stood wound down into the valley and lost itself amid the trees surrounding the Gate House, the car suddenly appeared again, and began to mount the slope toward us!

"Heavens!" whispered Carneta. "He may have seen us—with glasses! Quick! Let us walk back until the hill-top conceals us; then we must hide somewhere!"

I shared her excitement. Without a moment's hesitation we both turned and retraced our steps. Twenty paces brought us to a spot where a stack of mangel wurzels stood at the roadside.

"This will do!" I said.

We ran around into the field, and crouched where we could peer out on the road without ourselves being seen. Nor had we taken up this position a moment too soon.

Topping the slope came a light-weight electric, driven by a man who, in his spruce uniform, might have passed at a glance for a very dusky European. The car had a limousine back, and as the chauffeur slowed down, out from the open windows right and left peered the solitary occupant.

He had the cast of countenance which is associated with the best type of Jew, with clear-cut aquiline features wholly destitute of grossness. His white beard was patriarchal and he wore gold-rimmed pince-nez and a glossy silk hat. Such figures may often be met with in the great money-markets of the world, and Mr. Isaacs would have passed for a successful financier in even more discerning communities than that of Cadham.

But I scarcely breathed until the car was past; and, beside me, my companion, crouching to the ground, was trembling wildly. Fifty yards toward the village Mr. Isaacs evidently directed the man to return.

The car was put about, and flashed past us at high speed down into the valley. When the sound of the humming motor had died to something no louder than the buzz of a sleepy wasp, I held out my hand to Carneta and she rose, pale, but with blazing eyes, and picked up her camera case.

"If he had detected us, everything would have been lost!" she whispered.

"Not everything!" I replied grimly—and showed her the revolver which I had held in my hand whilst those eagle eyes had been seeking us. "If he had made a sign to show that he had seen us, in fact, if he had once offered a safe mark by leaning from the car, I should have shot him dead without hesitation!"

"We must not show ourselves again, but wait for dusk. He must have seen us, then, on the hilltop, but I hope without recognizing us. He has the sight and instincts of a vulture!"

I nodded, slipping the revolver into my pocket, but I wondered if I should not have been better advised to have risked a shot at the moment that I had recognized "Mr. Isaacs" for Hassan of Aleppo.

CHAPTER XXX
AT THE GATE HOUSE

From sunset to dusk I lurked about the neighbourhood of the Gate House with my beautiful accomplice—watching and waiting: a man bound upon stranger business, I dare swear, than any other in the county of Kent that night.

Our endeavour now was to avoid observation by any one, and in this, I think, we succeeded. At the same time, Carneta, upon whose experience I relied implicitly, regarded it as most important that we should observe (from a safe distance) any one who entered or quitted the gates.

But none entered, and none came out. When, finally, we made along the narrow footpath skirting the west of the grounds, the night was silent—most strangely still.

The trees met overhead, but no rustle disturbed their leaves and of animal life no indication showed itself. There was no moon.

A full appreciation of my mad folly came to me, and with it a sense of heavy depression. This stillness that ruled all about the house which sheltered the awful Sheikh of the Assassins was ominous, I thought. In short, my nerves were playing me tricks.

"We have little to fear," said my companion, speaking in a hushed and quivering voice. "The whole of the party left England some days ago."

"Are you sure?"

"Certain! We learned that before Earl made his attempt. Hassan remains, for some reason; Hassan and one other—the one who drives the car."

"But the slipper?"

"If Hassan remains, so does the slipper!" From the knapsack, which, as you will have divined, did not contain a camera, she took out an electric pocket lamp, and directed its beam upon the hedge above us.

"There is a gap somewhere here!" she said. "See if you can find it. I dare not show the light too long."

Darkness followed. I clambered up the bank and sought for the opening of which Carneta had spoken.

"The light here a moment," I whispered. "I think I have it!"

Out shone the white beam, and momentarily fell upon a black hole in the thickset hedge. The light disappeared, and as I extended my hand to Carneta she grasped it and climbed up beside me.

"Put on your rubber shoes," she directed. "Leave the others here."

There in the darkness I did as she directed, for I was provided with a pair of tennis shoes. Carneta already was suitably shod.

"I will go first," I said. "What is the ground like beyond?"

"Just unkempt bushes and weeds."

Upon hands and knees I crawled through, saw dimly that there was a short descent, corresponding with the ascent from the lane, and turned, whispering to my fellow conspirator to follow.

The grounds proved even more extensive than I had anticipated. We pressed on, dodging low-sweeping branches and keeping our arms up to guard our faces from outshoots of thorn bushes. Our progress necessarily was slow, but even so quite a long time seemed to have elapsed ere we came in sight of the house.

This was my first expedition of the kind; and now that my goal was actually in sight I became conscious of a sort of exultation hard to describe. My companion, on the contrary, seemed to have become icily cool. When next she spoke, her voice had a businesslike ring, which revealed the fact that she was no amateur at this class of work.

"Wait here," she directed. "I am going to pass all around the house, and I will rejoin you."

I could see her but dimly, and she moved off as silent as an Indian deer-stalker, leaving me alone there crouching at the extreme edge of the thicket. I looked out over a small wilderness of unkempt flower-beds; so much it was just possible to perceive. The plants in many instances had spread on to the pathways and contested survival with the flourishing weeds. All was wild—deserted—eerie.

A sense of dampness assailed me, and I raised my eyes to the low-lying building wherein no light showed, no sign of life was evident. The nearer wing presented a verandah apparently overgrown by some climbing plant, the nature of which it was impossible to determine in the darkness.

The zest for the nocturnal operation which temporarily had thrilled me succumbed now to loneliness. With keen anxiety I awaited the return of my more experienced accomplice. The situation was grotesque, utterly bizarre; but even my sense of humour could not save me from the growing dread which this seemingly deserted place poured into my heart.

When upon the right I heard a faint rustling I started, and grasped the revolver in my pocket.

"Not a sound!" came in Carneta's voice. "Keep just inside the bushes and come this way. There is something I want to show you."

The various profuse growths rendered concealment simple enough—if indeed any other concealment were necessary than that which the strangely black night afforded. Just within the evil-smelling thicket we made a half circuit of the building, and stopped.

"Look!" whispered Carneta.

The word was unnecessary, for I was staring fixedly in the direction of that which evidently had occasioned her uneasiness.

It was a small square window, so low-set that I assumed it to be that of a cellar, and heavily cross-barred.

From it, out upon a tangled patch of vegetation, shone a dull red light!

"There's no other light in the place," my companion whispered. "For God's sake, what can it be?"

My mind supplied no explanation. The idea that it might be a dark room no doubt was suggested by the assumed role of Carneta; but I knew that idea to be absurd. The red light meant something else.

Evidently the commencing of operations before all lights were out was irregular, for Carneta said slowly—

"We must wait and watch the light. There was formerly a moat around the Gate House; that must be the window of a dungeon."

I little relished the prospect of waiting in that swamp-like spot, but since no alternative presented itself I accepted the inevitable. For close upon an hour we stood watching the red window. No sound of bird, beast, or man disturbed our vigil; in fact, it would appear that the very insects shunned the neighbourhood of Hassan of Aleppo. But the red light still shone out.

"We must risk it!" said Carneta steadily. "There are French windows opening on to that verandah. Ten yards farther around the bushes come right up to the wall of the house. We'll go that way and around by the other wing on to the verandah."

Any action was preferable to this nerve-sapping delay, and with a determination to shoot, and shoot to kill, any one who opposed our entrance, I passed through the bushes and, with Carneta, rounded the southern border of that silent house and slipped quietly on to the verandah.

Kneeling, Carneta opened the knapsack. My eyes were growing accustomed to the darkness, and I was just able to see her deft hands at work upon the fastenings. She made no noise, and I watched her with an ever-growing wonder. A female burglar is a personage difficult to imagine. Certainly, no one ever could have suspected this girl with the violet eyes of being an expert crackswoman; but of her efficiency there could be no question. I think I had never witnessed a more amazing spectacle than that of this cultured girl manipulating the tools of the house breaker with her slim white fingers.

Suddenly she turned and clutched my arm.

"The windows are not fastened!" she whispered.

A strange courage came to me—perhaps that of desperation. For, ignoring the ominous circumstance, I pushed open the nearest window and stepped into the room beyond! A hissing breath from Carneta acknowledged my performance, and she entered close behind me, silent in her rubber-soled shoes.

For one thrilling moment we stood listening. Then came the white beam from the electric lamp to cut through the surrounding blackness.

The room was totally unfurnished!

CHAPTER XXXI
THE POOL OF DEATH

Not a sound broke the stillness of the Gate House. It was the most eerily silent place in which I had ever found myself. Out into the corridor we went, noiselessly. It was stripped, uncarpeted.

Three doors we passed, two upon the left and one upon the right. We tried them all. All were unfastened, and the rooms into which they opened bare and deserted. Then we came upon a short, descending stair, at its foot a massive oaken door.

Carneta glided down, noiseless as a ghost, and to one of the blackened panels applied an ingenious little instrument which she carried in her knapsack. It was not unlike a stethoscope; and as I watched her listening, by means of this arrangement, for any sound beyond the oaken door, I reflected how almost every advance made by science places a new tool in the hand of the criminal.

No word had been spoken since we had discovered this door; none had been necessary. For we both knew that the place beyond was that from which proceeded the mysterious red light.

I directed the ray of the electric torch upon Carneta, as she stood there listening, and against that sombre oaken background her face and profile stood out with startling beauty. She seemed half perplexed and half fearful. Then she abruptly removed the apparatus, and, stooping to the knapsack, replaced it and took out a bunch of wire keys, signing to me to hand her the lamp.

As I crept down the steps I saw her pause, glancing back over her shoulder toward the door. The expression upon her face induced me to direct the light in the same direction.

Why neither of us had observed the fact before I cannot conjecture; but a key was in the lock!

Perhaps the traffic of the night afforded no more dramatic moment than this. The house which we were come prepared burglariously to enter was thrown open, it would seem, to us, inviting our inspection!

Looking back upon that moment, it seems almost incredible that the sight of a key in a lock should have so thrilled me. But at the time I perceived something sinister in this failure of the Lord of the Hashishin to close his doors to intruders. That Carneta shared my doubts and fears was to be read in her face; but her training had been peculiar, I learned, and such as establishes a surprising resoluteness of character.

Quite noiselessly she turned the key, and holding a dainty pocket revolver in her hand, pushed the door open slowly!

An odour, sickly sweet and vaguely familiar, was borne to my nostrils. Carneta became outlined in dim, reddish light. Bending forward slightly, she entered the room, and I, with muscles tensed nervously, advanced and stood beside her.

I perceived that this was a cellar; indeed, I doubt not that in some past age it had served as a dungeon. From the stone roof hung the first evidence of Eastern occupation which the Gate House had yielded; in the form of an Oriental lantern, or fanoos, of rose-coloured waxed paper upon a copper frame. Its vague light revealed the interior of the hideous place upon whose threshold we stood.

Straight before us, deep set in the stone wall, was the tiny square window, iron-barred without, and glazed with red glass, the light from which had so deeply mystified us. Within a niche in the wall, a little to the left of the window, rested an object which, at that moment, claimed our undivided attention the sight of which so wrought upon us that temporarily all else was forgotten.

It was the red slipper of the Prophet!

"My God!" whispered Carneta—"my God!"—and clutched at me, swaying dizzily.

A few inches from our feet the floor became depressed, how deeply I could not determine, for it was filled with water, water filthy and slimy! The strange, nauseating odour had grown all but unsupportable; it seemingly proceeded from this fetid pool which, occupying the floor of the dungeon, offered a barrier, since its depth was unknown, of fully twelve feet between ourselves and the farther wall.

There was a faint, dripping sound: a whispering, echoing drip-drip of falling water. I could not tell from whence it proceeded.

Almost supporting my companion, whose courage seemed suddenly to have failed her, I stared fascinatedly at that blood-stained relic. Something then induced me to look behind; I suppose a warning instinct of that sort which is unexplainable. I only know that upholding Carneta with my left arm, and nervously grasping my revolver in my right, I turned and glanced over my shoulder.

Very slowly, but with a constant, regular motion, the massive door was closing!

I snatched away my arm; in my left hand I held the electric torch, and springing sharply about I directed the searching ray into the black gap of the stairway. A yellow face, a malignant Oriental face, came suddenly, fully, into view! Instantly I recognized it for that of the man who had driven Hassan's car!

Acting upon the determination with which I had entered the Gate House, I raised my revolver and fired straight between the evil eyes! To the fact that I dropped my left hand in the act of pulling the trigger with my right, and thus lost my mark, the servant of Hassan of Aleppo owed his escape. I missed him. He uttered a shrill cry of fear and went racing up the wooden stair. I followed him with the light and fired twice at the retreating figure. I heard him stumble and a second time cry out. But, though I doubt not he was hit, he recovered himself, for I heard his tread in the corridor above.

Propping wide the door with my foot, I turned to Carneta. Her face was drawn and haggard; but her mouth set in a sort of grim determination.

"Earl is dead!" she said, in a queer, toneless voice. "He died trying to get—that thing! I will get it, and destroy it!"

Before I could detain her, even had I sought to do so, she stepped into the filthy water, struggled to recover her foothold, and sank above her waist into its sliminess. Without hesitation she began to advance toward the niche which contained the slipper. In the middle of the pool she stopped.

What memory it was which supplied the clue to the identity of that nauseating smell, heaven alone knows; but as the girl stopped and drew herself up rigidly—then turned and leapt wildly back toward the door—I knew what occasioned that sickly odour!

She screamed once, dreadfully—shrilly—a scream of agonizing fear that I can never forget. Then, roughly I grasped her, for the need was urgent—and dragged her out on to the floor beside me. With her wet garments clinging to her limbs, she fell prostrate on the stones.

A yard from the brink the slimy water parted, and the yellow snout of a huge crocodile was raised above the surface! The saurian eyes, hungrily malevolent, rose next to view!

The extremity of our danger found me suddenly cool. As the thing drew its slimy body up out of the poor I waited. The jaws were extended toward the prostrate body, were but inches removed from it, dripped their saliva upon the soddened skirt—when I bent forward, and at a range of some ten inches emptied the remaining three loaded chambers of my revolver into the creature's left eye!

Upchurned in bloody foam became the water of that dreadful place.... As one recalls the incidents of a fevered dream, I recall dragging Carneta away from the contorted body of the death-stricken reptile. A nightmare chaos of horrid, revolting sights and sounds forms my only recollection of quitting the dungeon of the slipper.

I succeeded in carrying her up the stairs and out through the empty rooms on to the verandah; but there, from sheer exhaustion, I laid her down. I had no means of reviving her and I lacked the strength to carry her farther. Having recharged my revolver, I stood watching her where she lay, wanly beautiful in the dim light.

There was no doubt in my mind respecting the fate of Earl Dexter, nor could I doubt that the slipper in the dungeon below was a duplicate of the real one. It was a death-trap into which he had lured Dexter and which he had left baited for whomsoever might trace the cracksman to the Gate House. Why Hassan should have remained behind, unless from fanatic lust of killing, I could not imagine.

When at last the fresher night air had its effect, and Carneta opened her eyes, I led her to the gates, nor did she offer the slightest resistance, but looked dully before her, muttering over and over again, "Earl, Earl!"

The gates were open; we passed out on to the open road. No man pursued us, and the night was gravely still.

CHAPTER XXXII
SIX GRAY PATCHES

When the invitation came from my old friend Hilton to spend a week "roughing it" with him in Warwickshire I accepted with alacrity. If ever a man needed a holiday I was that man. Nervous breakdown threatened me at any moment; the ghastly experience at the Gate House together with Carneta's grief-stricken face when I had parted from her were obsessing memories which I sought in vain to shake off.

A brief wire had contained the welcome invitation, and up to the time when I had received it I had been unaware that Hilton was back in England. Moreover, beyond the fact that his house, "Uplands," was near H—, for which I was instructed to change at New Street Station, Birmingham, I had little idea of its location. But he added "Wire train and will meet at H—"; so that I had no uneasiness on that score.

I had contemplated catching the 2:45 from Euston, but by the time I had got my work into something like order, I decided that the 6:55 would be more suitable and decided to dine on the train.

Altogether, there was something of a rush and hustle attendant upon getting away, and when at last I found myself in the cab, bound for Euston, I sat back with a long-drawn sigh. The quest of the Prophet's slipper was ended; in all probability that blood-stained relic was already Eastward bound. Hassan of Aleppo, its awful guardian, had triumphed and had escaped retribution. Earl Dexter was dead. I could not doubt that; for the memory of his beautiful accomplice, Carneta, as I last had seen her, broken-hearted, with her great violet eyes dulled in tearless agony—have I not said that it lived with me?

Even as the picture of her lovely, pale face presented itself to my mind, the cab was held up by a temporary block in the traffic—and my imagination played me a strange trick.

Another taxi ran close alongside, almost at the moment that the press of vehicles moved on again. Certainly, I had no more than a passing glimpse of the occupants; but I could have sworn that violet eyes looked suddenly into mine, and with equal conviction I could have sworn to the gaunt face of the man who sat beside the violet-eyed girl for that of Earl Dexter!

The travellers, however, were immediately lost to sight in the rear, and I was left to conjecture whether this had been a not uncommon form of optical delusion or whether I had seen a ghost.

At any rate, as I passed in between the big pillars, "The gateway of the North," I scrutinized, and closely, the numerous hurrying figures about me. None of them, by any stretch of the imagination, could have been set down for that of Dexter, The Stetson Man. No doubt, I concluded, I had been tricked by a chance resemblance.

Having dispatched my telegram, I boarded the 6:55. I thought I should have the compartment to myself, and so deep in reverie was I that the train was actually clear of the platforms ere I learned that I had a companion. He must have joined me at the moment that the train started. Certainly, I had not seen him enter. But, suddenly looking up, I met the eyes of this man who occupied the corner seat facing me.

This person was olive-skinned, clean-shaven, fine featured, and perfectly groomed. His age might have been anything from twenty-five to forty-five, but his hair and brows were jet black. His eyes, too, were nearer to real black than any human eyes I had ever seen before—excepting the awful eyes of Hassan of Aleppo. Hassan of Aleppo! It was, to that hour, a mystery how his group of trained assassins—the Hashishin—had quitted England. Since none of them were known to the police, it was no insoluble mystery, I admit; but nevertheless it was singular that the careful watching of the ports had yielded no result. Could it be that some of them had not yet left the country? Could it be—

I looked intently into the black eyes. They were caressing, smiling eyes, and looked boldly into mine. I picked up a magazine, pretending to read. But I supported it with my left hand; my right was in my coat pocket—and it rested upon my Smith and Wesson!

So much had the slipper of Mohammed done for me: I went in hourly dread of murderous attack!

My travelling companion watched me; of that I was certain. I could feel his gaze. But he made no move and no word passed between us. This was the situation when the train slowed into Northampton. At Northampton, to my indescribable relief (frankly, I was as nervous in those days as a woman), the Oriental traveller stepped out on to the platform.

Having reclosed the door, he turned and leaned in through the open window.

"Evidently you are not concerned, Mr. Cavanagh," he said. "Be warned. Do not interfere with those that are!"

The night swallowed him up.

My fears had been justified; the man was one of the Hashishin—a spy of Hassan of Aleppo! What did it mean?

I craned from the window, searching the platform right and left. But there was no sign of him.

When the train left Northampton I found myself alone, and I should only weary you were I to attempt to recount the troubled conjectures that bore me company to Birmingham.

The train reached New Street at nine, with the result that having gulped a badly needed brandy and soda in the buffet, I grabbed my bag, raced across— and just missed the connection! More than an hour later I found myself standing at ten minutes to eleven upon the H— platform, watching the red taillight of the "local" disappear into the night. Then I realized to the full that with four miles of lonely England before me there hung above my head a mysterious threat—a vague menace. The solitary official, who but waited my departure to lock up the station, was the last representative of civilization I could hope to encounter until the gates of "Uplands" should be opened to me!

What was the matter with which I was warned not to interfere? Might I not, by my mere presence in that place, unwittingly be interfering now?

With the station-master's directions humming like a refrain in my ears, I passed through the sleeping village and out on to the road. The moon was exceptionally bright and unobscured, although a dense bank of cloud crept slowly from the west, and before me the path stretched as an unbroken thread of silvery white twining a sinuous way up the bracken-covered slope, to where, sharply defined against the moonlight sky, a coppice in grotesque silhouette marked the summit.

The month had been dry and tropically hot, and my footsteps rang crisply upon the hard ground. There is nothing more deceptive than a straight road up a hill; and half an hour's steady tramping but saw me approaching the trees.

I had so far resolutely endeavoured to keep my mind away from the idea of surveillance. Now, as I paused to light my pipe—a never-failing friend in loneliness—I perceived something move in the shadows of a neighbouring bush.

This object was not unlike a bladder, and the very incongruity of its appearance served to revive all my apprehensions. Taking up my grip, as though I had noticed nothing of an alarming nature, I pursued my way up the slope, leaving a trail of tobacco smoke in my wake; and having my revolver secreted up my right coat-sleeve.

Successfully resisting a temptation to glance behind, I entered the cover of the coppice, and, now invisible to any one who might be dogging me, stood and looked back upon the moon-bright road.

There was no living thing in sight, the road was empty as far as the eye could see. The coppice now remained to be negotiated, and then, if the station-master's directions were not at fault, "Uplands" should be visible beyond. Taking, therefore, what I had designed to be a final glance back down the hillside, I was preparing to resume my way when I saw something—something that arrested me.

It was a long way behind—so far that, had the moon been less bright, I could never have discerned it. What it was I could not even conjecture; but it had the appearance of a vague gray patch, moving—not along the road, but through the undergrowth—in my direction.

For a second my eye rested upon it. Then I saw a second patch—a third—a fourth!

Six!

There were six gray patches creeping up the slope toward me!

The sight was unnerving. What were these things that approached, silently, stealthily—like snakes in the grass?

A fear, unlike anything I had known before the quest of the Prophet's slipper had brought fantastic horror into my life, came upon me. Revolver in hand I ran—ran for my life toward the gap in the trees that marked the coppice end. And as I went something hummed through the darkness beside my head, some projectile, some venomous thing that missed its mark by a bare inch!

Painfully conversant with the uncanny weapons employed by the Hashishin, I knew now, beyond any possibility of doubt, that death was behind me.

A pattering like naked feet sounded on the road, and, without pausing in my headlong career, I sent a random shot into the blackness.

The crack of the Smith and Wesson reassured me. I pulled up short, turned, and looked back toward the trees.

Nothing—no one!

Breathing heavily, I crammed my extinguished briar into my pocket—re-charged the empty chamber of the revolver—and started to run again toward a light that showed over the treetops to my left.

That, if the man's directions were right, was "Uplands"—if his directions were wrong—then...

A shrill whistle—minor, eerie, in rising cadence—sounded on the dead silence with piercing clearness! Six whistles—seemingly from all around me—replied!

Some object came humming through the air, and I ducked wildly.

On and on I ran—flying from an unknown, but, as a warning instinct told me, deadly peril—ran as a man runs pursued by devils.

The road bent sharply to the left then forked. Overhanging trees concealed the house, and the light, though high up under the eaves, was no longer visible. Trusting to Providence to guide me, I plunged down the lane that turned to the left, and, almost exhausted, saw the gates before me—saw the sweep of the drive, and the moonlight, gleaming on the windows!

None of the windows were illuminated.

Straight up to the iron gates I raced.

They were locked!

Without a moment's hesitation I hurled my grip over the top and clambered up the bars! As I got astride, from the blackness of the lane came the ominous hum, and my hat went spinning away across the lawn!—the black cloud veiled the moon and complete darkness fell.

Then I dropped and ran for the house—shouting, though all but winded—"Hilton! Hilton! Open the door!"

Sinking exhausted on the steps, I looked toward the gates—but they showed only dimly in the dense shadows of the trees.

Bzzz! Buzz!

I dropped flat in the portico as something struck the metal knob of the door and rebounded over me. A shower of gravel told of another misdirected projectile.

Crack! Crack! Crack! The revolver spoke its short reply into the mysterious darkness; but the night gave up no sound to tell of a shot gone home.

"Hilton! Hilton!" I cried, banging on the panels with the butt of the weapon. "Open the door! Open the door!"

And now I heard the coming footsteps along the hall within; heavy bolts were withdrawn—the door swung open—and Hilton, pale-faced, appeared. His hand shot out, grabbed my coat collar; and weak, exhausted, I found myself snatched into safety, and the door rebolted.

"Thank God!" I whispered. "Thank God! Hilton, look to all your bolts and fastenings. Hell is outside!"

CHAPTER XXXIII
HOW WE WERE REINFORCED

Hilton, I learned, was living the simple life at "Uplands." The place was not yet decorated and was only partly furnished. But with his man, Soar, he had been in solitary occupation for a week.

"Feel better now?" he asked anxiously.

I reached for my tumbler and blew a cloud of smoke into the air. I could hear Soar's footsteps as he made the round of bolts and bars, testing each anxiously.

"Thanks, Hilton," I said. "I'm quite all right. You are naturally wondering what the devil it all means? Well, then, I wired you from Euston that I was coming by the 6:55."

"H— Post Office shuts at 7. I shall get your wire in the morning!"

"That explains your failing to meet me. Now for my explanation!"

"Surrounding this house at the present moment," I continued, "are members of an Eastern organization—the Hashishin, founded in Khorassan in the eleventh century and flourishing to-day!"

"Do you mean it, Cavanagh?"

"I do! One Hassan of Aleppo is the present Sheikh of the order, and he has come to England, bringing a fiendish company in his train, in pursuit of the sacred slipper of Mohammed, which was stolen by the late Professor Deeping—-"

"Surely I have read something about this?"

"Probably. Deeping was murdered by Hassan! The slipper was placed in the Antiquarian Museum—"

"From which it was stolen again!"

"Correct—by Earl Dexter, America's foremost crook! But the real facts have never got into print. I am the only pressman who knows them, and I have good reason for keeping my knowledge to myself! Dexter is dead (I believe I saw his ghost to-day). But although, to the best of my knowledge, the accursed slipper is in the hands of Hassan and Company, I have been watched since I left Euston, and on my way to 'Uplands' my life was attempted!"

"For God's sake, why?"

"I cannot surmise, Hilton. Deeping, for certain reasons that are irrelevant at the moment, left the keys of the case at the Museum in my perpetual keeping—but the case was rifled a second time—"

"I read of it!"

"And the keys were stolen from me. I am utterly at a loss to understand why the Hashishin—for it is members of that awful organization who, without a doubt, surround this house at the present moment—should seek my life. Hilton, I have brought trouble with me!"

"It's almost incredible!" said Hilton, staring at me. "Why do these people pursue you?"

Ere I had time to reply Soar entered, arrayed, as was Hilton, in his night attire. Soar was an ex-dragoon and a model man.

"Everything fast, sir," he reported; "but from the window of the bedroom over here—the room I got ready for Mr. Cavanagh—I thought I saw someone in the orchard."

"Eh?" jerked Hilton—"in the orchard? Come on up, Cavanagh!"

We all ran upstairs. The moonlight was streaming into the room.

"Keep back!" I warned.

Well within the shadow, I crept up to the window and looked out. The night was hot and still. No breeze stirred the leaves, but the edge of the frowning thunder cloud which I had noted before spread a heavy carpet of ebony black upon the ground. Beyond, I could dimly discern the hills. The others stood behind me, constrained by the fear of this mysterious danger which I had brought to "Uplands."

There was someone moving among the trees!

Closer came the figure, and closer, until suddenly a shaft of moonlight found passage and spilled a momentary pool of light amid the shadows, I could see the watcher very clearly. A moment he stood there, motionless, and looking up at the window; then as he glided again into the shade of the trees the darkness became complete. But I watched, crouching there nervously, for long after he was gone.

"For God's sake, who is it?" whispered Hilton, with a sort of awe in his voice.

"It's Hassan of Aleppo!" I replied.

Virtually, the house, with the capital of the Midlands so near upon the one hand, the feverish activity of the Black Country reddening the night upon the other, was invested by fanatic Easterns!

We descended again to the extemporized study. Soar entered with us and Hilton invited him to sit down.

"We must stick together to-night!" he said. "Now, Cavanagh, let us see if we can find any explanation of this amazing business. I can understand that at one period of the slipper's history you were an object of interest to those who sought to recover it; but if, as you say, the Hashishin have the slipper now, what do they want with you? If you have never touched it, they cannot be prompted by desire for vengeance."

"I have never touched it," I replied grimly; "nor even any receptacle containing it."

As I ceased speaking came a distant muffled rumbling.

"That's the thunder," said Hilton. "There's a tremendous storm brewing."

He poured out three glasses of whisky, and was about to speak when Soar held up a warning finger.

"Listen!" he said.

At his words, with tropical suddenness down came the rain.

Hilton, his pipe in his hand, stood listening intently.

"What?" he asked.

"I don't know, sir; the sound of the rain has drowned it."

Indeed, the rain was descending in a perfect deluge, its continuous roar drowning all other sounds; but as we three listened tensely we detected a noise which hitherto had seemed like the overflowing of some spout.

But louder and clearer it grew, until at last I knew it for what it was.

"It's a motor-car!" I cried.

"And coming here!" added Soar. "Listen! it's in the lane!"

"It certainly isn't a taxicab," declared Hilton. "None of the men will come beyond the village."

"That's the gate!" said Soar, in an awed voice, and stood up, looking at Hilton.

"Come on," said the latter abruptly, making for the door.

"Be careful, Hilton!" I cried; "it may be a trick!"

Soar unbolted the front door, threw it open, and looked out. In the darkness of the storm it was almost impossible to see anything in the lane outside. But at that moment a great sheet of lightning split the gloom, and we saw a taxicab standing close up to the gateway!

"Help! Open the gate!" came a high-pitched voice; "open the gate!"

Out into the rain we ran and down the gravel path. Soar had the gate open in a twinkling, and a woman carrying a brown leather grip, but who was so closely veiled that I had no glimpse of her features, leapt through on to the drive.

"Lend a hand, two of you!" cried a vaguely familiar voice—"this way!"

Hilton and Soar stepped out into the road. The driver of the cab was lying forward across the wheel, apparently insensible, but as Hilton seized his arm he moved and spoke feebly.

"For God's sake be quick, sir!" he said. "They're after us! They're on the other side of the lane, there!"

With that he dropped limply into Hilton's arms!

He was dragged in on to the drive—and something whizzed over our heads and went sputtering into the gravel away up toward the house. The last to enter was the man who had come in the cab. As he barred the gate behind him he suddenly reached out through the bars and I saw a pistol in his hand.

Once—twice—thrice—he fired into the blackness of the lane.

"Take that, you swine!" he shouted. "Take that!"

As quickly as we could, bearing the insensible man, we hurried back to the door. On the step the woman was waiting for us, with her veil raised. A blinding flash of lightning came as we mounted the step—and I looked into the violet eyes of Carneta! I turned and stared at the man behind me.

It was Earl Dexter.

Three of the mysterious missiles fell amongst us, but miraculously no one was struck. Amid the mighty booming of the thunder we reentered the houses and got the door barred. In the hall we laid down the unconscious man and stood, a strangely met company, peering at one another in the dim lamplight.

"We've got to bury the hatchet, Mr. Cavanagh!" said Dexter. "It's a case of the common enemy. I've brought you your bag!" and he pointed to the brown grip upon the floor.

"My bag!" I cried. "My bag is upstairs in my room."

"Wrong, sir!" snapped The Stetson Man. "They are like as two peas in a pod, I'll grant you, but the bag you snatched off the platform at New Street was mine! That's what I'm after; I ought to be on the way to Liverpool. That's what Hassan's after!"

"The bag!"

"You don't need to ask what's in the bag?" suggested Dexter.

"What is in the bag?" ask Hilton hoarsely.

"The slipper of the Prophet, sir!" was the reply.

CHAPTER XXXIV
MY LAST MEETING WITH HASSAN OF ALEPPO

I felt dazed, as a man must feel who has just heard the death sentence pronounced upon him. Hilton seemed to have become incapable of speech or action; and in silence we stood watching Carneta tending the unconscious man. She forced brandy from a flask between his teeth, kneeling there beside him with her face very pale and dark rings around her eyes. Presently she looked up.

"Will you please get me a bowl of water and a sponge?" she said quietly.

Soar departed without a word, and no one spoke until he returned, bringing the sponge and the water, when the girl set to work in a businesslike way to cleanse a wound which showed upon the man's head.

"She's a good nurse is Carneta," said Dexter coolly. "She was the only doctor I had through this"—indicating his maimed wrist. "If you will fetch my bag down, there's some lint in it."

I hesitated.

"You needn't worry," said Dexter; "as well be hung for a sheep as a lamb. You've handled the bag, and I'm not asking you to do any more."

I went up to my room and lifted the grip from the chair upon which I had put it. Even now I found it difficult to perceive any difference between this and mine. Both were of identical appearance and both new. In fact, I had bought mine only that morning, my old one being past use, and being in a hurry, I had not left it to be initialled.

As I picked up the bag the lightning flashed again, and from the window I could see the orchard as clearly as by sunlight. At the farther end near the wall someone was standing watching the house.

I went downstairs carrying the fatal bag, and rejoined the group in the hall.

"He will have to be got to bed," said Carneta, referring to the wounded man; "he will probably remain unconscious for a long time."

Accordingly, we took the patient into one of the few furnished bedrooms, and having put him to bed left him in care of the beautiful nurse. When we four men met again downstairs, amazement had rendered the whole scene unreal to me. Soar stood just within the open door, not knowing whether to go or to remain; but Hilton motioned to him to stay. Earl Dexter bit off the end of a cigar and stood with his left elbow resting on the mantelpiece.

His gaunt face looked gaunter than ever, but the daredevil gray eyes still nursed that humorous light in their depths.

"Mr. Cavanagh," he said, "we're brothers! And if you'll consider a minute, you'll see that I'm not lying when I say I'm on the straight, now and for always!"

I made no reply: I could think of none.

"I'm a crook," he resumed, "or I was up to a while ago. There's a warrant out for me—the first that ever bore my name. I've sailed near the wind often enough, but it was desperation that got me into hot water about that!"

He jerked his cigar in the direction of his grip, which lay now on the rug at his feet.

"I lost a useful right hand," he went on—"and I lost every cent I had. It was a dead rotten speculation—for I lost my good name! I mean it! Believe me, I've handled some shady propositions in the past, but I did it right in the sunlight! Up to the time I went out for that damned slipper I could have had lunch with any detective from Broadway to the Strand! I didn't need any false whiskers and the Ritz was good enough for The Stetson Man. What now? I'm 'wanted!' Enough said."

He tossed the cigar—he had smoked scarce an inch of it—into the empty grate.

"I'm an Aunt Sally for any man to shy at," he resumed bitterly. "My place henceforth is in the dark. Right! I've finished; the book's closed. From the time I quit England—if I can quit—I'm on the straight! I've promised Carneta, and I mean to keep my word. See here—"

Dexter turned to me.

"You'll want to know how I escaped from the cursed death-trap at Hassan's house in Kent? I'll tell you. I was never in it! I was hiding and waiting my chance. You know what was left to guard the slipper while the Sheikh—rot him—was away looking after arrangements for getting his mob out of the country?"

I nodded.

"You fell into the trap—you and Carneta. By God! I didn't know till it was all over! But two minutes later I was inside that place—and three minutes later I was away with the slipper! Oh, it wasn't a duplicate; it was the goods! What then? Carneta had had a sickening of the business and she just invited me to say Yes or No. I said Yes; and I'm a straight man onward."

"Then what were you doing on the train with the slipper?" asked Hilton sharply.

"I was going to Liverpool, sir!" snapped The Stetson Man, turning on him. "I was going to try to get aboard the Mauretania and then make terms for my life! What happened? I slipped out at Birmingham for a drink—grip in hand! I put it down beside me, and Mr. Cavanagh here, all in a hustle, must have rushed in behind me, snatched a whisky and snatched my grip and started for H—!"

A vivid flash of lightning flickered about the room. Then came the deafening boom of the thunder, right over the house it seemed.

"I knew from the weight of the grip it wasn't mine," said Dexter, "and I was the most surprised guy in Great Britain and Ireland when I found whose it was! I opened it, of course! And right on top was a waistcoat and right in the first pocket was a telegram. Here it is!"

He passed it to me. It was that which I had received from Hilton. I had packed the suit which I had been wearing that morning and must previously have thrust the telegram into the waistcoat pocket.

"Providence!" Dexter assured me. "Because I got on the station in time to see Hassan of Aleppo join the train for H—! I was too late, though. But I chartered a taxi out on Corporation Street and invited the man to race the local! He couldn't do it, but we got here in time for the fireworks! Mr. Cavanagh, there are anything from six to ten Hashishin watching this house!"

"I know it!"

"They're bareheaded; and in the dark their shaven skulls look like nothing human. They're armed with those damned tubes, too. I'd give a thousand dollars—if I had it!—to know their mechanism. Well, gentlemen, deeds speak. What am I here for, when I might be on the way to Liverpool, and safety?"

"You're here to try to make up for the past a bit!" said a soft, musical voice. "Mr. Cavanagh's life is in danger."

Carneta entered the room.

The light played in that wonderful hair of hers; and pale though she was, I thought I had never seen a more beautiful woman.

"Tell them," she said quietly, "what must be done."

Soar glanced at me out of the corner of his eyes and shifted uneasily. Hilton stared as if fascinated.

"Now," rapped Dexter, in his strident voice, "putting aside all questions of justice and right (we're not policemen), what do we want—you and I, Mr. Cavanagh?"

"I can't think clearly about anything," I said dully. "Explain yourself."

"Very well. Inspector Bristol, C.I.D., would want me and Hassan arrested. I don't want that! What I want is peace; I want to be able to sleep in comfort; I want to know I'm not likely to be murdered on the next corner! Same with you?"

"Yes—yes."

"How can we manage it? One way would be to kill Hassan of Aleppo; but he wants a lot of killing—I've tried! Moreover, directly we'd done it, another Sheikh-al-jebal would be nominated and he'd carry on the bloody work. We'd be worse off than ever. Right! we've got to connive at letting the blood-stained fanatic escape, and we've got to give up the slipper!"

"I'll do that with all my heart!"

"Sure! But you and I have both got little scores up against Hassan, which it's not in human nature to forget. But I've got it worked out that there's only one way. It may nearly choke us to have to do it, I'll allow. I'm working on the Moslem character. Mr. Hilton, make up a fire in the grate here!"

Hilton stared, not comprehending.

"Do as he asks," I said. "Personally, I am resigned to mutilation, since I have touched the bag containing the slipper, but if Dexter has a plan—"

"Excuse me, sir," Soar interrupted. "I believe there's some coal in the coal-box, but I shall have to break up a packing-case for firewood—or go out into the yard!"

"Let it be the packing-case," replied Hilton hastily.

Accordingly a fire was kindled, whilst we all stood about the room in a sort of fearful uncertainty; and before long a big blaze was roaring up the chimney. Dexter turned to me.

"Mr. Cavanagh," said he, "I want you to go right upstairs, open a first-floor window—I would suggest that of your bedroom—and invite Hassan of Aleppo to come and discuss terms!"

Silence followed his words; we were all amazed. Then—

"Why do you ask me to do this?" I inquired.

"Because," replied Dexter, "I happen to know that Hassan has some queer kind of respect for you—I don't know why."

"Which is probably the reason why he tried to kill me to-night!"

"That's beside the question, Mr. Cavanagh. He will believe you—which is the important point."

"Very well. I have no idea what you have in mind but I am prepared to adopt any plan since I have none of my own. What shall I say?"

"Say that we are prepared to return the slipper—on conditions."

"He will probably try to shoot me as I stand at the window."

Dexter shrugged his shoulders.

"Got to risk it," he drawled.

"And what are the conditions?"

"He must come right in here and discuss them! Guarantee him safe conduct and I don't think he'll hesitate. Anyway, if he does, just tell him that the slipper will be destroyed immediately!"

Without a word I turned on my heel and ascended the stairs.

I entered my room, crossed to the window, and threw it widely open. Hovering over the distant hills I could see the ominous thunder cloud, but the storm seemed to have passed from "Uplands," and only a distant muttering with the faint dripping of water from the pipes broke the silence of the night. A great darkness reigned, however, and I was entirely unable to see if any one was in the orchard.

Like some mueddin of fantastic fable I stood there.

"Hassan!" I cried—"Hassan of Aleppo!"

The name rang out strangely upon the stillness—the name which for me had a dreadful significance; but the whole episode seemed unreal, the voice that had cried unlike my voice.

Instantly as any magician summoning an efreet I was answered.

Out from the trees strode a tall figure, a figure I could not mistake. It was that of Hassan of Aleppo!

"I hear, effendim, and obey," he said. "I am ready. Open the door!"

"We are prepared to discuss terms. You may come and go safely"—still my voice sounded unfamiliar in my ears.

"I know, effendim; it is so written. Open the door."

I closed the window and mechanically descended the stairs.

"Mind it isn't a trap!" cried Hilton, who, with the others, had overheard every word of this strange interview. "They may try to rush the door directly we open it."

"I'll stand the chest behind it," said Soar; "between the door and the wall, so that only one can enter at a time."

This was done, and the door opened.

Alone, majestic, entered Hassan of Aleppo.

He was dressed in European clothes but wore the green turban of a Sherif. With his snowy beard and coal-black eyes he seemed like a vision of the Prophet, of the Prophet in whose name he had committed such ghastly atrocities.

Deigning no glance to Soar nor to Hilton, he paced into the room, passing me and ignoring Carneta, where Earl Dexter awaited him. I shall never forget the scene as Hassan entered, to stand looking with blazing eyes at The Stetson Man, who sat beside the fire with the slipper of Mohammed in his hand!

"Hassan," said Dexter quietly, "Mr. Cavanagh has had to promise you safe conduct, or as sure as God made me, I'd put a bullet in you!"

The Sheikh of the Hashishin glared fixedly at him.

"Companion of the evil one," he said, "it is not written that I shall die by your hand—or by the hand of any here. But it has been revealed to me that to-night the gates of Paradise may be closed in my face."

"I shouldn't be at all surprised," drawled Dexter. "But it's up to you. You've got to swear by Mohammed—"

"Salla-'llahu 'aleyhi wasellem!"

"That you won't lay a hand upon any living soul, or allow any of your followers to do so, who has touched the slipper or had anything to do with it, but that you will go in peace."

"You are doomed to die!"

"You don't agree, then?"

"Those who have offended must suffer the penalty!"

"Right!" said Dexter—and prepared to toss the slipper into the heart of the fire!

"Stop! Infidel! Stop!"

There was real agony in Hassan's voice. To my inexpressible surprise he dropped upon his knee, extending his lean brown hands toward the slipper.

Dexter hesitated. "You agree, then?"

Hassan raised his eyes to the ceiling.

"I agree," he said. "Dark are the ways. It is the will of God…"

Dimly the booming of the thunder came echoing back to us from the hills. Above its roll sounded a barbaric chanting to which the drums of angry heaven formed a fitting accompaniment.

I heard Soar shooting the bolts again upon the going of our strange visitor.

Faint and more faint grew the chanting, until it merged into the remote muttering of the storm—and was lost. The quest of the sacred slipper was ended.